EXPLORE BRITAIN'S
STEAM
RAILWAYS

Produced by AA Publishing

$\mathscr{E}$XPLORE $\mathscr{B}$RITAIN'S

$\mathscr{S}$TEAM $\mathscr{R}$AILWAYS

by Anthony Lambert

Foreword by Christopher Awdry

The author would like to thank the preserved railways for their invaluable help in the preparation of this book.

The extract on p12–14 from *Lines of Character* by LTC Rolt is reproduced by kind permission of Constable & Company Limited.

Copy Editor: Penny Hicks

Published by AA Publishing, a trading name of Automobile Association Developments Limited, whose registered office is Norfolk House, Priestley Road, Basingstoke, Hampshire RG24 9NY. Registered Number 1878835.

A catalogue record for this book is available from the British Library.

ISBN   h/b 0 7495 1050 1
          p/b 0 7495 1790 5

Colour origination by L.C. Repro and Sons Ltd, Aldermaston.
Printed and bound by Graficromo SA, Spain.

The contents of this book are believed correct at the time of printing. Nevertheless, the Publishers cannot accept responsibility for errors or omissions, or for changes in details given.

Telephone numbers
Through 1999 and 2000 telephone numbers will be changed as follows:
London – 020 code replaces 0171 and 0181, local numbers become eight-digit by adding 7 to the beginning of inner London numbers and 8 to outer London numbers.
Southampton and Portsmouth – 023 code replaces 01703 and 01705, local numbers become eight-digit by adding 80 to the beginning of Southampton numbers and 92 to Portsmouth numbers.
Coventry – 024 code replaces 01203, local numbers become eight-digit by adding 76 to the beginning of numbers.
Cardiff – 029 code replaces 01222, local numbers become eight-digit by adding 20 to the beginning of numbers.

The Automobile Association wishes to thank the following photographers and libraries for their assistance in the preparation of this book.

AA PHOTO LIBRARY with contributions from; front cover J. Mottershaw, back cover P. Aithie, spine A. Tryner, 9 M. Birkitt, 10 S & O Matthews, 12 D. Forss, 13 F. Stephenson, 14/5 A. Baker, 15 M. Birkitt, 16 D. Forss, 17 S & O Matthews, 18/9, 19 R. Moss, 20, 21 I. Burgum, 22/3 E. Meacher, 23 N. Ray, 24/5, 25 F. Stephenson, 26/7 R. Moss, 27 D. Croucher, 28/9, 29, 30, 32, 33a, 33b, 34, 35 R. Moss, 36 J. Mottershaw, 37 R. Elliott, 38/9, 39 D. Jackson, 40, 41, 42/3, 43 N. Ray, 44 D. Forss, 44/5 P. Brown, 46, 47 D. Forss, 48, 49 W. Voysey, 50 C. Lees, 51 W. Voysey, 52, 53, 54, 54/5 D. Forss, 58/9 W. Voysey, 60/1, 61 D. Croucher, 62, 63, 64 , 65 D. Forss, 66, 67 A. Tryner, 68/9, 69 M. Birkitt, 70/1, 71 A. Tryner, 72 R. Newton, 72/3 , 74 A. Tryner, 75 R. Newton, 76 J. Beazley, 77a S & O Matthews, 78, 79, 80, 81 A. Tryner, 82/2, 83 M. Birkitt, 84/5, 85 R. Edwards, 86/7, 87 P. Aithie, 88/9, 89 I. Burgum, 90/1, 91, 92/3, 93, 94 P. Aithie 94/5 J. Mottershaw, 95 R. Moss, 97, 96/7 I. Burgum, 98, 99, 100, 101, 102, 103, 104, 105a, 105b P. Aithie, 106/7, 107, 108/9, 109 F. Stephenson, 110/1 R. Newton, 111 I. Burgum, 112 R. Newton, 113 M. Allwood-Coppin, 114/5, 115 I. Burgum, 116, 117, 118, 119a, 119b R. Newton, 120/1, 121, 122, 122/3 J. Mottershaw, 124, 125, 126 V. Bates, 127, 128/9 J. Mottershaw, 129 R. Newton, 130 J. Mottershaw, 131 A. Baker, 132/3, 133 C. Lees, 134 C. Molyneux, 135 V. Patel, 136/7, 137, 138, 138/9 J. Mottershaw, 140/1, 141, 142/3, 143 C. Lees, 144 S. King, 145, 146, 147a, 147b C. Lees, 148, 149 J. Mottershaw, 150/1, 151 M. Alexander, 152, 153 M. Taylor, 154/5, 155 E. Bowness, 156, 157 S. Day, 158/9, 159 J. Henderson
ROD KERRY 11 Flying Scotsman, 56 Watercress Line, Ropley, 57 Watercress Line, Ropley, 59 Watercress Line, Medstead
MARY EVANS PICTURE LIBRARY 36 Newcastle Central Station, 108 Newcastle Central, 159 Kings Cross

CONTENTS

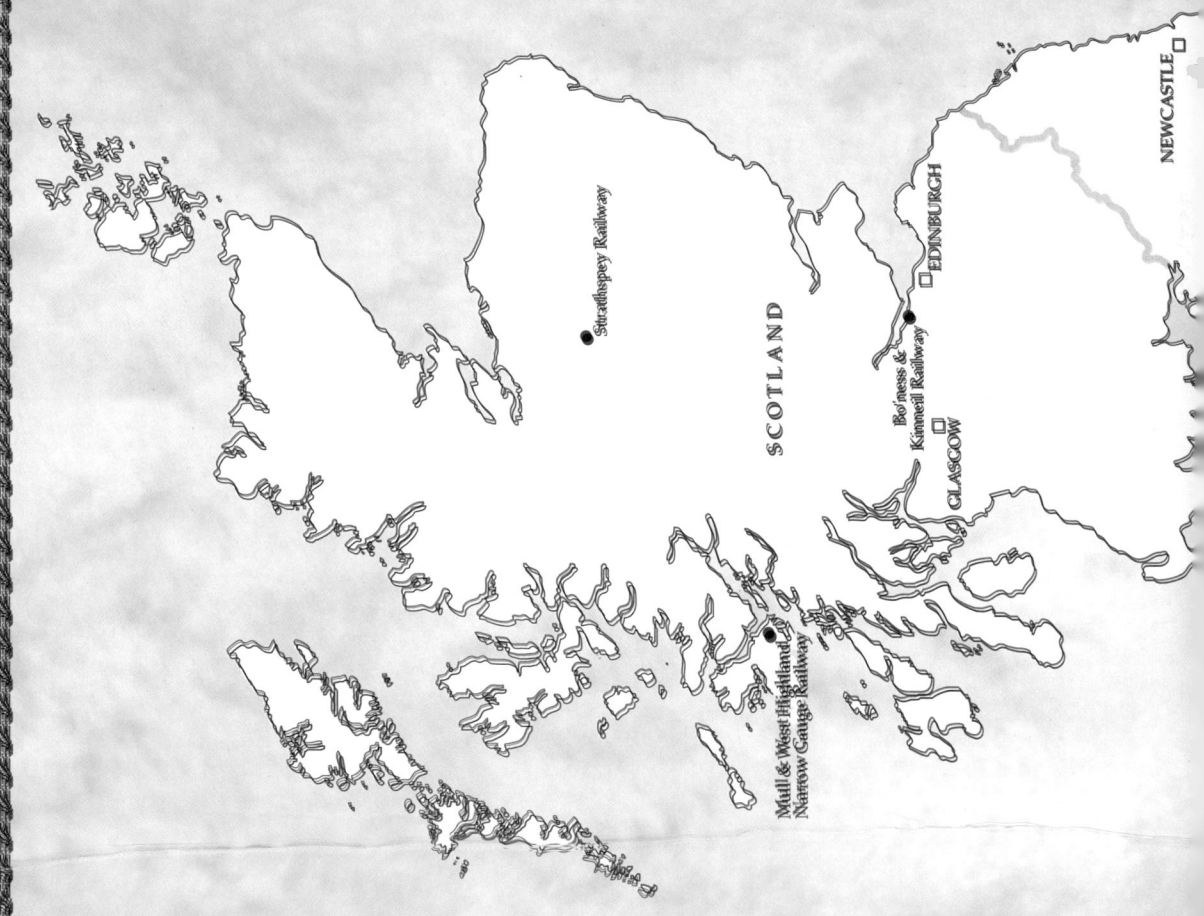

Explore Britain's Steam Railways

Location Map

Strathspey Railway

SCOTLAND

Bo'ness & Kinneil Railway

EDINBURGH

GLASGOW

Mull & West Highland Narrow Gauge Railway

NEWCASTLE

NORTH
COUNTRY

North Yorkshire
Moors Railway

Ravenglass &
Eskdale Railway

Lakeside & Haverthwaite
Railway

Isle of Man
Steam Railway

Keighley & Worth
Valley Railway

East Lancashire
Railway

LEEDS

MANCHESTER

North Norfolk
Railway

Bure Valley
Railway

NORWICH

Midland Railway
Centre

Great Central
Railway

The Battlefield
Line

Nene Valley
Railway

CENTRAL ENGLAND

AND EAST ANGLIA

SOUTH AND

SOUTH-EAST

LONDON

ENGLAND

Kent & East Sussex
Railway

Romney, Hythe &
Dymchurch Railway

Bluebell
Railway

Isle of Wight
Steam Railway

Mid-Hants
Railway

Swanage
Railway

Foxfield Steam
Railway

BIRMINGHAM

Severn Valley
Railway

Llangollen
Railway

Welshpool &
Llanfair Railway

Llanberis Lake
Railway

Bala Lake
Railway

Snowdon Mountain
Railway

Ffestiniog
Railway

Talyllyn Railway

Vale of Rheidol
Railway

WALES

AND THE

MARCHES

Brecon Mountain
Railway

Dean Forest
Railway

Gwili Railway

CARDIFF

Gloucestershire
Warwickshire
Railway

BRISTOL

East Somerset
Railway

West Somerset
Railway

WEST

COUNTRY

Launceston
Steam Railway

South Devon
Railway

Paignton & Dartmouth
Steam Railway

Bodmin & Wenford
Railway

0   20   40   60   80   100 miles

0   40   80   120   160 km

OREWORD

---

by Christopher Awdry

Not very long ago the railway was the only method of transport that the general public could use in order to reach the countryside. The growth of motor transport and consequent contraction of the railway system have now made this less effective, but, almost as if in reaction, we find ourselves with a growing number of 'preserved' lines, each trying to recreate the atmosphere of the heyday of the railways.

Roads, in holiday areas particularly, now become so choked with traffic that the steam railway offers a welcome day away from them. Not only that, but the railways will often carry their passengers – I don't think any of them will call you a 'customer' – not just for a ride, but in a leisurely and enjoyable way to the seaside, to a local beauty spot or stately home, or to a tourist attraction of some sort.

This book covers 40 of the best-known lines, including the one on which my father and I cut our preservation teeth more than forty years ago. The Talyllyn Railway then, as has often been told, was in a very run-down state, the rails held in place more by faith and the surrounding turf

than by any mechanical means. Now it is a smart, friendly and well-run line, and it is a source of some pride to me that in 1994 my son began his Guard's training there as soon as he was legally old enough to do so.

Ours is not a unique story, for those first steps in preservation taken on the Talyllyn in the early 1950s have snowballed into what has become a major leisure market. Forty five years on there are more than 200 steam centres dotted around the United Kingdom, most of them depending on volunteers for survival. Some are commercially orientated, others have more to offer in the way of extra attractions. What is not in doubt is that each railway has its own unique atmosphere, its own dedicated volunteers and that each offers a chance to slow the pace of our hectic life for a while.

Every railway within these pages can be recommended, and the variety they offer is remarkable. So sit back and enjoy this overview. When you've done that, why not sample a few of the lines for yourselves, relaxing as the scenery drifts past outside the carriage window, with, just for once, the train taking the strain.

Taking control on the Isle of Wight Steam Railway

$\mathscr{I}$NTRODUCTION

▸◂

team railways are a major part of Britain's tourist industry. Each year over 6.5 million passengers travel on them, and their combined turnover is about £15m. Their appeal lies principally in the perennial fascination of the steam locomotive, which writers, painters, composers and photographers have tried to express and explain since the first spirited eulogies were written about the iron horse in the early 19th century.

Of course, there were those like Ruskin and Wordsworth who abhorred the steam locomotive and what railways were doing to the look of the country – but then they hadn't seen a motorway. Children are in no two minds about them, the popularity of Thomas the Tank Engine days on preserved railways reflecting the unprecedented sales of the Reverend W Awdry's books and associated merchandise. And for adults the steam

The Flying Scotsman *on the Swanage Railway*

railway is associated, perhaps, with a time when there were more certainties and continuities in our lives than in today's ceaseless preoccupation with change.

How did the idea of saving steam railways begin? Rather improbably it started with a meeting in Birmingham, called by the late L T C Rolt in a letter to *The Times*, inviting anyone with a will to save the narrow gauge Talyllyn Railway in Wales to be at the Imperial Hotel on a day in October 1950. Enough people turned up, formed a committee and the Talyllyn Railway Preservation Society was born. For an explanation of their motives, one can do no better than quote Rolt, arguably

the most poetic writer with a profound appreciation of the appeal of steam in the landscape, whether applied to railways, canals or agriculture:

'For the romantic the speed and power of the steam train epitomises the freedom and romance of travel, while the whole atmosphere of the railway is magic; the sulphurous echoing gloom of a great station at night, with signal lamps and other mysterious lights glowing and flickering over the intricate mesh of rails beyond the platform faces where steam drifts and buffers clash; the hot summer's day somnolence of some remote country station suddenly awakened to expectancy by the single beat of a bell

Below: Sheffield Park signal box, the Bluebell Railway

Opposite: changing the lamps on the Gloucestershire Warwickshire Railway

*Restoration work in progress
at Haworth, headquarters
of the Keighley & Worth
Valley Railway*

in the signal box; the whine of the wind in the telegraph wires on a lonely upland section as we wait to watch the passing of a northbound express. Yet at the same time the classicist within us is aware that this romance is in fact the by-product of order and discipline; that a great railway system is perhaps the most elaborate and delicate, yet at the same time one of the most successful feats of organisation ever evolved by man. The steel rail is a symbol of disciplined movement, but that movement is itself ordered and controlled by a complex human and mechanical hierarchy which extends from the central control room to the loneliest lineside signal box and which has made the railway the safest form of transport ever evolved.'

Whether or not they would have articulated their feelings in the way Rolt did, sufficient people, both as volunteers and as passengers, felt the same emotional and rational attachment to the steam railway as he did. Fortunately the Talyllyn rescue was successful. Had the Talyllyn rescue bid failed, Britain might not have gone on to reclaim more preserved railways per square mile than any other country in the world. Its success encouraged others to tackle the first standard gauge railway, the Bluebell, in 1960, and soon schemes were springing up everywhere. Some were unrealistic, echoing the wilder fantasies of the mid 19th-century railway manias; others were soundly based and managed. But there were a few voices urging caution, suggesting that the cake was finite and that every new scheme cut it more thinly.

One reason for the proliferation of proposals was the attachment felt to particular pre-grouping or pre-nationalisation companies. Before the creation of British Railways in 1948, there were four large railway companies: the Great Western, London Midland & Scottish, London & North Eastern and

Part of the Nene Valley
Railway's extensive collection
of locomotives, including
Thomas, *named by the*
Reverend W Awdry

Southern. Each was distinctive in character, locomotive and rolling stock liveries and in the areas they served. They had been created in 1922 by the government-decreed 'grouping' of over 140 railway companies of very different size into the 'Big Four', as the post-grouping companies were called. The first phase of railway preservation was often concerned to re-create the ambiance of one of these companies.

Another reason was the desire to have a *local* preserved railway, as opposed to one in the next county. Sometimes the ambition has been simply to cover costs and fund repairs, but most preserved railways have had to develop an increasingly professional outlook, becoming significant businesses in the local economy of smaller towns. Most have had to dilute the early ideal of volunteer labour with a nucleus of paid staff, particularly to cope with locomotive maintenance and driving.

Finding sufficient volunteers to run services that operate on weekdays during the summer months has become increasingly difficult.

Part of the problem has been the need to diversify to increase income, in turn creating a requirement for a core of paid staff. Faced with a need to provide better maintenance facilities, more covered accommodation or undertake costly repairs to an ageing viaduct or tunnel, railways have had to generate more income than can be found through the fare box. Catering and retailing have been obvious extensions of their core activity, but many have added contract engineering services for locomotives, retail wholesaling and corporate entertainment to augment income. None the less, without the loyal support of volunteers and periodic injections of capital through share issues, few preserved railways would survive for long.

Top-quality maintenance on the Bluebell Railway

They do so because they give pleasure – to those who travel on them and to those who often devote hundreds of hours a year to their chosen railway. Volunteers come from all walks of life and often undertake work wholly re-moved from their normal occupations, though the help of those with specialist engineering skills is particularly valued. It is to them that the greatest thanks are due for the continuance of the sight and sounds of the steam railway.

Locomotion *on display at the Darlington Railway Museum*

BODMIN & WENFORD RAILWAY

Cornwall

BODMIN, 16 MILES (25 KM) WEST OF LISKEARD

*T*he Bodmin & Wenford Railway offers a unique opportunity to compare the most modern of rail services with the nostalgia of the age of steam. It is the only preserved railway which is served by 125mph (200kph) High Speed Trains, and after being whisked from London Paddington or Edinburgh, passengers can cross a covered footbridge at Bodmin Parkway to an island platform from which Bodmin & Wenford trains depart. The 3½-mile (5.5 km) line, originally opened by the Great Western Railway in 1887, is the only standard gauge preserved railway in Cornwall, and recalls the days when the county was served by a fine network of picturesque branch lines to many of the principal resorts and market towns.

As the branch line turns away from the main line, it crosses a five-arch viaduct across the River Fowey, which rises on Bodmin Moor, then begins a taxing climb through wooded cuttings towards the one intermediate stop at

Passing Charlie's Gate

Colesloggett Halt. This was built by the Bodmin & Wenford to serve a network of paths created by the Forestry Commission through nearby Cardinham Woods. The railway's guide book contains a description and a map of the woods showing the four routes through them; cycles can be hired at the entrance and refreshments are available at an adjacent café.

The climb continues through banks of bracken and foxgloves with fine views northwards over the fields to Bodmin Moor. On the outskirts of Bodmin the railway's largest steam locomotive, Southern Railway West Country class No 34007 *Wadebridge*, may be glimpsed on the east side, undergoing restoration beside the Fitzgerald Lighting factory. A little farther on are the redundant barracks of the Duke of Cornwall's Light Infantry. In 1944 the railway brought Field Marshall Montgomery and General Eisenhower to visit the regiment.

As the train enters the station after the 25-minute slog uphill (it takes only 20 minutes going back), a line swings in from the left. This was a link to Boscarne Junction and Wadebridge, which the Bodmin & Wenford hopes to re-open in order to to relieve local roads of china clay lorries as well as to take passengers to the Camel Trail. The attractive terminus at Bodmin is a 25-minute walk from the start of this popular trail which extends for 15 miles (24km) to the sea at Padstow. Cycles can be hired in Wadebridge, which is linked by bus to Bodmin and Padstow.

Train service: Easter daily; April Wednesday and Sunday; May and October Tuesday, Wednesday and Sunday; June to September daily. Santa specials. Tel: 01208 73666.

Fireman at work on Swiftsure, a 1943 Hunslet

DEAN FOREST RAILWAY
Gloucestershire

LYDNEY, 9 MILES (14.5 KM) NORTH-EAST OF CHEPSTOW

Coal and iron ore have been mined in the Forest of Dean since before Roman times. By the late 18th century crude waggonways were being built to transport the minerals out of the forest, and some of these were later converted into steam-worked railways. The line of the Dean Forest Railway was one of them. It started as a horse-drawn tramway in 1810, built by the Severn & Wye Railway, and was gradually converted to steam traction and railway standards. The 3½-mile (5km) section operated by the Dean Forest Railway is the last of innumerable lines into the Forest, and runs from Lydney Junction to Norchard, where the main centre has been established.

That simple description belies the Herculean task of its creation on the site of a colliery that once employed 400 men. By the time the Dean Forest Railway began work, both colliery and railway were returning to the forest, calling for navvying on a scale seldom equalled in preservation. All buildings had disappeared, so every structure has had to be located, bought, dismantled, transported and re-erected: a signal box from Gloucester, a platform from Chippenham, a station building from deeper in the forest. Equally, the Dean Forest's engines have had to be restored from a dire condition, and its principal locomotive, a gleaming black Great Western Railway Pannier tank, is another resurrection from the scrapyard at Barry (see page 32).

As trains edge into the thickly wooded valley the scenery is redolent of an older England, before such large expanses of deciduous forests were felled for development, bisected by motorways or reduced in size to become country parks, shorn of their natural state. The Dean Forest Railway

Concentration on the footplate

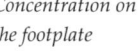

hopes to extend further into the forest to Parkend and perhaps beyond, which will permit many to reach walks in the Forest without use of cars. There is also the prospect of the line reaching the Dean Heritage Centre through the fourth oldest railway tunnel in the country, if not the world – the 1064yd (973m) long Haie Tunnel, which opened in 1809.

Train service: Sundays from April to October; also Wednesdays from June to August. Santa specials. Tel: 01594 843423.

GWR Pannier tank No 9681 (built in 1949) rounding a bend

EAST SOMERSET RAILWAY
Somerset

CRANMORE, 2½ MILES (4 KM) EAST OF SHEPTON MALLET

Most preserved railways are the result of a shared vision which drives widely different people to pool their skills. The East Somerset Railway, however, was the brainchild of just one man – and he holds elephants responsible. In 1967 the wildlife painter David Shepherd had just sold all his paintings of elephants on exhibition in New York when the opportunity arose to indulge his other passion – steam railways – by buying one of British Rail's last steam locomotives. Naturally he needed somewhere to keep it, along with the other locomotives he was later to acquire, and this 2-mile (3km) line is the result of a long search.

The main station is at Cranmore, where there is a connection with Railtrack through a line which was once part of the Great Western Railway branch from Witham to Yatton via Shepton Mallet and Wells, though today it is used only for stone traffic. The station building at Cranmore is the only original station remaining on the entire branch, though the signal box, of later date, has survived to become a museum, with an art gallery displaying David Shepherd's work on its upper floor.

The railway has a strong environmental theme, which is immediately apparent to visitors: a wildlife information centre adjoins the car park, and beside the station is a British-built engine which saw service in Zambia and was presented to David Shepherd by President Kaunda in recognition of his work on behalf of African wildlife. The lush pasture and woods through which the line passes are home to badgers, foxes and deer, and the deep Doulting Cutting abounds with ancient fossils, for which it has been designated a Site of Special Scientific Interest.

The 12-minute journey can be broken at the halt provided for picnickers at Merryfield Lane on the outward journey, or at Cranmore West on the return. The halt here enables you to walk through the marvellous replica of a Great Western Railway

engine shed and admire the well-equipped workshops from a viewing platform. Here the East Somerset's eight steam locomotives are overhauled. They range from the huge freight locomotive, *Black Prince*, to the tiny industrial tanks, *Lord Fisher* and *Lady Nan*, and include a rare crane tank from a steelworks in Staffordshire.

Train service: all year on selected days. Santa specials. Tel: 01749 880417.

Lady Nan, *in blue and red livery (left and below) was built in 1920*

GLOUCESTERSHIRE WARWICKSHIRE RAILWAY
Gloucestershire

TODDINGTON, 7 MILES (11 KM) NORTH-EAST OF CHELTENHAM

*T*here seems no limit to the achievements – and ambitions – of railway preservationists. The Gloucestershire Warwickshire Railway (the other GWR) started with nothing more than a trackless railway route, with few surviving buildings between Broadway and Cheltenham Racecourse. It has already re-opened 6 miles (9.5 km) of the line, and its ultimate goal is to buy further freeholds to enable it to run all the way to Stratford-upon-Avon, where the line originally met the surviving commuter route to Birmingham. To rebuild the existing line between the headquarters at Toddington and Far Stanley, volunteers have had to rebuild platforms, dismantle all manner of buildings and

artefacts for re-erection and set up facilities for the repair and maintenance of locomotives and carriages – none of the stations on the route even had an engine shed.

Before leaving on the 50-minute return journey, passengers can visit Toddington station's added attraction of the 2ft (610mm) gauge North Gloucestershire Railway – a railway within a railway – which offers rides behind a German engine; others from Natal and Poland can be seen under restoration.

The railway runs south from Toddington through the picturesque Vale of Evesham, awash with apple and fruit blossom in spring. The produce of the orchards was once a

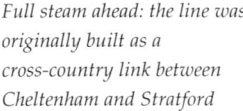
Full steam ahead: the line was originally built as a cross-country link between Cheltenham and Stratford

major source of traffic for the railway, which was closed by British Rail in 1977. Running parallel with the line to the east is the Cotswold escarpment, its limestone providing the lovely honey-coloured stone that is used for many of the district's buildings.

In the lea of the ridge are the remains of the 13th-century Hailes Abbey, once served by a halt on the railway. Beyond the hamlet of Didbrook the observant eye can discern remnants of the medieval strip farming system, denoted by long rectangles of raised ground. Another charming sight is provided by the goats which are used to keep down the grass on embankments and cuttings – infinitely preferable to spraying with chemicals. The goats are farmed by a local Gloucestershire Warwickshire Railway member.

Winchcombe station building stood at Monmouth (Troy) until it was dismantled and each stone numbered to assist re-erection. As the train pulls away from this popular Cotswold town, it enters a cutting leading to Greet Tunnel, at 693yds (633m) the second longest on a preserved

railway. The line stops in the middle of the country, pending extension, but the short wait while the locomotive runs round is no hardship in such surroundings.

Train service: steam: weekends from end March to early September, Sundays only to early October; also diesel on selected days during Easter week and summer holidays, and Sundays in November. Santa and other family specials. Tel: 01242 621405.

Toddington station, where the North Gloucestershire Railway is also based

Miniature
Railways

*Queen of Nebraska of
Dobwalls Forest Railroad
being cleaned*

Four of Britain's longest miniature railways are featured separately, but there are dozens of other miniature railways, ranging from short end-to-end lines to complex interwoven railways with runs of a mile or more. Examples of these masterpieces of compression may be found on the Forest Railroad at Dobwalls, where one of the largest

steam locomotives ever built, the *Union Pacific Big Boy*, is reproduced for a 7¼in (184mm) gauge line. It takes several trips to fathom the layout, thanks to the ingenuity of its design. Footpaths take visitors to viewing points where a succession of US goliaths-in-miniature pass by with trains of 30–40 people. The Moors Valley Railway, in the country park near Ringwood, is equally ambitious. Of the same gauge, it gives the feel of a busy main line during holiday periods, when several trains are running and the signal boxes are necessary rather than just decorative. The main station has an overall roof that adds to the atmosphere of a main line in miniature, and doubles as a carriage shed.

The Conwy Valley Railway at Betws-y-Coed, and Gorse Blossom Farm railways both have delightful settings, in the latter case twisting through the Devonshire woodland in deep cuttings, tunnels or bridges. At Betws-y-Coed, the line runs parallel with the scenic main line from Llandudno Junction to Blaenau Ffestiniog, through the foothills of Snowdonia. The Audley End Railway in Essex is perhaps the best-known of a number of railways that operate at country houses, running on estate farmland so as not to detract from the garden. Another notable example, at Weston Park in Shropshire, features a viaduct over part of a lake.

The Fairbourne & Barmouth is probably the most original of the many seaside railways. Built on the route of a much older line, this unique 12¼in (311mm) line has some very fine models of narrow gauge prototypes running through tunnels amid the sand dunes of the Mawddach estuary. Another seaside line is Norfolk's Wells & Walsingham, built on the trackbed of a British Railways branch line, and providing a public transport link as well as a pleasurable ride.

An unusual line operates on Sundays during the summer for the benefit of charities. The Great Cockrow Railway at Chertsey, in Surrey, was founded by the transport publisher Ian Allan and is run by a group of volunteers, rather like a standard gauge preserved railway. It has state-of-the-art electronic as well as mechanical signalling, which is vital for the safe control of four or five moving trains.

Fun for all the family at Frimley Lodge Park, Surrey

The railway at Launceston steams through some of Cornwall's loveliest scenery

LAUNCESTON STEAM RAILWAY
Cornwall

LAUNCESTON, 10 MILES (16 KM) WEST OF TAVISTOCK

The tranquil countryside of north Cornwall may seem a strange place to see at work a collection of enchanting narrow gauge locomotives that spent their working lives in the slate quarries of north Wales. Their presence here was the result of the encouraging response given by the local authority to the idea of building a railway for them on the trackbed of the line that once carried the Atlantic Coast Express.

Opened in stages since 1983, the Launceston Steam Railway offers more than a 2-mile (3.2 km) journey along the broad valley of the River Kensey – it is also a skilful bringing together of buildings and fixtures from far and wide, many of which have fascinating associations. The café and booking hall was originally a three-bedroomed bungalow at Cranleigh in Surrey that had been on show at the first Ideal Home Exhibition in 1919, and sheltering passengers on the platform outside is the canopy from nearby Tavistock North station. Adjacent is a large stone building once used by the

Launceston Gas Company, the ground floor of which is now the British Engineering Exhibition, housing stationary steam engines. One of the engines here was used by a hospital near Hitchin to drive water pumps and laundry machinery. Above them, reached by a staircase rescued from New Cross Hospital in London, is a collection of vintage cars and motorcycles.

The tall-funnelled quarry engines are nearly all centenarians and products of Hunslet in Leeds. They amble along, taking 40 minutes for the round trip, although visitors can stop off at Hunts Crossing for a picnic beside the river – through the kindness of the farmer who owns the field. The area is a haven for wildlife, and passengers may be lucky enough to see woodpeckers, buzzards and herons, while the railway banks are known to be home to rabbits, stoats, badgers, lizards, adders and grass snakes.

Beyond Hunts Crossing the valley opens up, affording wider views over the farmland. The line currently stops in the middle of nowhere; passengers can get down while the engine runs round the train and view the trackbed that will become the extension to the hamlet of New Mills. Looking along the overgrown route, it is hard to imagine the holiday expresses packed with excited holidaymakers which once rushed through the valley on their way from London Waterloo and Exeter to Wadebridge and Padstow.

Train service: daily except Saturdays from Whitsun until September. Tuesdays and Sundays from Easter and in October. Santa specials. Tel: 01566 775665.

Launceston station, where there are vintage cars and motorcycles, stationary steam engines and an exhibition of model railways to be seen

PAIGNTON & DARTMOUTH STEAM RAILWAY

Devon

PAIGNTON, 3 MILES (5KM) NORTH OF TORQUAY

Because of their relatively short extent, preserved railways can seldom offer very different landscapes from the carriage window, but one exception is the Paignton & Dartmouth Steam Railway. It begins amidst the candyfloss of Paignton town centre, runs along the cliffs overlooking Torbay before turning inland for a mile or two of pastoral Devon, and finishes with one of the most lovely sections of railway in the

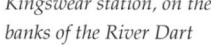

Kingswear station, on the banks of the River Dart

country as the line drops down to sea level beside the wooded estuary of the River Dart.

This line was once part of Brunel's broad gauge (7ft/2.13m) Great Western Railway, leaving the West of England main line to the south of Newton Abbot station and serving Torquay en route. After conversion to standard gauge, it became the destination of the Torbay Express from London Paddington, but the final 7 miles (11km) no longer provided the financial returns expected by British Rail. They were closed in 1972, only to be re-opened in the same year by an offshoot of the Dart Valley Railway.

At Paignton the lines of Railtrack and the Paignton & Dartmouth had to be separated, although through excursion trains can still be transferred and the interchange between the two is very easy. The trains of the Paignton & Dartmouth still evoke the character of the Great Western, with its Middle Green locomotives and chocolate and cream coaches, although most of the carriages are of later manufacture. The steep gradients of the line mean that powerful locomotives have to be used except during the quieter parts of the year.

All the railway's steam engines are of GWR ancestry, the most powerful being a heavy tank locomotive built

originally for south Wales coal trains. No 5239, named *Goliath* by the Paignton & Dartmouth, was built in 1924 and rescued from a huge collection of locomotives once stored for scrap at Barry in south Wales. In the event, only a handful were cut up, the majority being bought for use on preserved railways. Many were badly corroded and missing vital parts, making their return to service a tribute to the tenacity and skill of volunteers and the few paid engineers on railways all over Britain.

A pair of tender locomotives, No 7827 *Lydham Manor* and No 4920 *Dumbleton Hall*, were also rescued from Barry, but one of two 45XX class tank engines, No 4555, was bought while still in service on British Railways. Other small tank engines are unlikely to be seen on service trains, being too underpowered for the gradients. Their steepness is apparent soon after leaving Paington. The journey starts by travelling past what is left of Goodrington carriage sidings, recalling the days when the West Country would receive hundreds of special trains every summer weekend. As the sea comes into view to the east, the train passes Goodrington platform and the line begins the climb to Churston at gradients of 1 in 60/70. While the engine barks away at the front, passengers enjoy a magnificent view over the beaches towards Torquay.

After crossing the stone viaducts at Broadsands and Hookhills, the line begins to turn inland, pausing at Churston from where a branch line used to run off to the fishing port of Brixham. On the right is the railway's maintenance shed. From here the line begins its descent to the sea, twisting through woods and fields to the 497yd (454m) Greenway Tunnel, one of the longest on a preserved railway.

Those travelling the line for the first time are astonished by the wholly different landscape that appears as the train bursts out of the southern portal, for the tunnel takes the train into the estuary of the Dart. You get your first glimpse of the river as the train drops down from the curve of Greenway Viaduct. The trees thin out to reveal hundreds of tiny boats and the odd naval vessel anchored beneath the imposing Britannia Royal Naval College, built in 1905 and attended by many royal princes.

If the station at Kingswear seems familiar, it could be because it was used for the railway scenes in the film of *The French Lieutenant's Woman*. Ferries cross the harbour at two points to the larger town of Dartmouth, where a modest building on the waterfront covers one of the country's oldest stationary steam engines – a pump engine for a local mine, built by the Dartmouth ironmonger Thomas Newcomen in 1711.

A range of tickets is available for the half-hour single journey, so that passengers can take the ferry across the harbour or include an excursion on the River Dart, perhaps returning by bus from Totnes to Paignton.

Train service: selected dates April, May and October; daily from May to September. Santa specials. Tel: 01803 555872.

GWR 2-6-2T No. 4588 steaming along the coast near Goodrington

Left, waiting at Paignton station

Below, Dumbleton Hall, *dating from 1929, was rescued from Barry, in Wales*

With its many tourist attractions, Buckfastleigh station (above and opposite) is the line's most popular starting point

SOUTH DEVON RAILWAY
Devon

BUCKFASTLEIGH, 11 MILES (17.5 KM) WEST OF PAIGNTON

Originally known as the Dart Valley Railway, this line is seldom out of view of the River Dart during the 25-minute journey. It is one of the prettiest stretches of the river valley and can be appreciated to the full only from the train, since few roads thread the valley and glimpses of the river are rare. The water is home to salmon and trout, so the lucky passenger might catch sight of a salmon leaping its way up-river to spawn. Flying over the water you may see ducks, swans, herons or even a kingfisher, and beside the line is a profusion of primroses and wild daffodils in spring. If time permits, alight at the lovely intermediate station at Staverton, star of many a film. From here, as from Totnes station, there are pleasant walks to be enjoyed along the river.

In common with other tourist railways in the West Country, the South Devon Railway relies upon holidaymakers for most of its traffic, but no other line began its second life in the way that this one did. The Dart Valley Railway was set up by a group of businessmen who believed that the former Great Western Railway branch line from Totnes to Ashburton could be run as a commercial enterprise, and that a volunteer workforce would not be crucial to its operation. However, a vital section of the line north of the intermediate station at Buckfastleigh disappeared for ever under the new A38 trunk road, restricting re-opening in 1969 to the southern 7 miles (11km). The company soon acquired the Paignton & Dartmouth Railway, which became its principal interest, and today the South Devon Railway is leased from them by new operators who do rely on volunteer labour.

Most passengers join the trains at the Buckfastleigh end of the line, which is easy to reach from the A38, has a large car park and is handy for a number of other tourist attractions. But Totnes has much to recommend it too, and visitors without a car can easily get to the terminus here by public transport – a new footbridge was opened in 1993 linking Littlehempston (Totnes) station with the town centre and main line station.

Train service: daily from June to the end of September, Wednesdays and most weekends in April, May and October. Santa specials. Tel: 01364 642338.

Railway
Architecture

It has not been the primary purpose of preserved railways to protect outstanding examples of railway architecture, but some railways have inevitably inherited structures that are exceptional or even listed (denoting statutory protection) when they took over their lines. For example, the Severn Valley Railway took on responsibility for the listed 1861 Victoria Bridge across the River Severn. However, in most instances such buildings have been bought by or given to the preserved railways and physically moved from their original location. Some were under threat of demolition; others were deteriorating, unused and would soon have been beyond repair.

Examples of re-erected buildings can be found throughout this book, but of special note are the unique train shed rescued from Haymarket station in Edinburgh for the Bo'ness & Kinneil Railway, the high standard of work in rebuilding Foulridge station on the Keighley & Worth Valley Railway, and the transhipment shed at Didcot Railway Museum in which goods were once transferred from broad gauge to standard gauge wagons.

Since 1979 encouragement in the

While the Keighley & Worth Valley Railway inherited its original buildings, below, many railways rely on station buildings painstakingly re-erected far from their first home

care of buildings has been given to preserved railways by the Ian Allan Railway Heritage Awards. These are organised by the Association of Railway Preservation Societies and supported by Railtrack, Westinghouse Brake & Signal Ltd and the Railway Heritage Trust. Various categories exist, some applying to Railtrack stations as well as the preserved sector. Some railways fortunate enough to have good buildings, and which have restored them well, have won a number of awards – nearly all the original stations on the Keighley & Worth Valley, for example, have won awards at least once.

The railways are not the only custodians of good buildings. A number of museums have been set up in former railway buildings, ranging from the Royalty & Empire exhibition at Windsor & Eton Central to the small station at Errol near Perth, which was restored as a museum of local railway history by a trust set up in the town. Some of these buildings are of listed status, such as Monkwearmouth near Sunderland and Darlington North Road in which the Darlington Railway Centre has been set up. It is one of the oldest surviving stations, dating from 1842, and it contains a collection of locomotives, carriages and relics relating to the railways of the north-east.

Amongst the most important railway buildings surviving anywhere in the world are those around the original terminus of the Liverpool & Manchester Railway, in Manchester itself. Opened in 1830, the railway was a landmark in transport history, and the station and goods warehouse have been cleverly incorporated in the Museum of Science and Industry.

Sheringham, the North Norfolk Railway's elegant main station

SWANAGE RAILWAY
Dorset

SWANAGE, 10 MILES (16 KM) SOUTH OF BOURNEMOUTH

The existence of the Swanage Railway, one of Britain's most attractive steam railways, represents a triumph of local opinion over the recommendations of the district council. The council had acquired the site for redevelopment, but before their plans were put into action, they decided to ask the inhabitants of the seaside town whether they would prefer the station to re-open. The townspeople voted overwhelmingly in favour of the station, and so began the reconstruction of the picturesque branch that had once opened up the previously remote Isle of Purbeck in 1885.

The line has gradually been rebuilt from Swanage, through Harman's Cross and the famous village of Corfe Castle and on to the present terminus at Norden. Today it not only provides a delightful journey through the Purbeck countryside, but also helps to relieve pressure on the traffic-choked village of Corfe Castle and the busy town of Swanage. Most of the railway buildings had survived, though the tracks had to be relaid, and because the bridges along the line were designed to carry heavy express locomotives – Swanage once had an express service to London Waterloo – its trains are once again hauled by such large locomotives as a Bulleid Light Pacific.

Swanage station has been wonderfully restored to its 1930s appearance, from the colour of the paintwork on its period buildings to its enamel advertising signs, and the increasingly

Enthusiasts chatting to the driver of the Flying Scotsman

rare sight of semaphore signals contribute to the atmosphere. It takes about 45 minutes for the 6-mile (9.5 km) journey to Norden, but most travellers break the journey somewhere along the way, either to visit Corfe Castle, with its stirring Civil War history and evocative castle ruins, or to enjoy one of the fine walks around Purbeck, particularly on the escarpment to the north which is rich in early remains, including the Iron Age fort of Badbury Rings.

Train service: daily throughout the year (but not Saturdays in January and early February). Santa specials. Tel: 01929 425800.

Swanage station. The railway is also known as the Purbeck Line

WEST SOMERSET RAILWAY
Somerset

BISHOPS LYDEARD, 5 MILES (8 KM) NORTH-WEST OF TAUNTON

Stretching for 20 miles (32km) between Bishops Lydeard and Minehead, the West Somerset Railway is the longest preserved railway in Britain. It may one day be even longer, for there is still a connection with the main line to the west of Taunton station for the occasional through excursion. For the time being, however, passengers arriving by train at Taunton are usually met by a connecting bus which takes them to the eastern terminus at Bishops Lydeard.

The existence of this railway is due to the initiative of the county council,

Bishops Lydeard station

The smart cream and chocolate-brown paintwork of the railway's coaches

which purchased the line following its closure by British Rail in 1971. This enabled the West Somerset Railway to refurbish the route and re-open it in stages between 1976 and 1979. It retains the atmosphere of a Great Western Railway single-track holiday branch – indeed it became so busy during the summer months that two special passing loops had to be built to break up sections between stations, and the platform at Minehead was lengthened to accommodate 16-coach trains. This legacy has stood the railway in good stead, for it needs to run long trains during the peak holiday season to cope with the volume of travellers. Passengers at Bishops Lydeard have plenty to occupy their time, for there is a visitor centre in the former goods shed, incorporating a locomotive or coach, a working signalbox and signals, photographs, railway memorabilia and a model railway.

Northbound trains have a stiff climb for 4 miles (6.5km) to the highest point of the line at Crowcombe Heathfield, where the station has two platforms and a separate stationmaster's house with decorative bargeboards. Views of the Quantock and Brendon Hills open up to the left before arrival at Stogumber, seemingly a good example of minimalist station design, with its tiny platform shelter – in fact the station building is unusually positioned at ground level on the opposite side of the track to the platform. At this station passengers can take advantage of a picnic site in lovely surroundings. The half-way station of Williton has two architectural delights for connoisseurs of industrial buildings – it has the only surviving operational Bristol & Exeter Railway signal box, and a very early metal-framed prefabricated structure which was dismantled at Swindon

The line near Crowcombe, which has one of the railway's ten stations

railway works and re-erected here. A listed building, it now provides covered accommodation for rolling stock.

Beyond Williton the train comes within 15yds (13m) of the sea at high tide, and as it approaches Watchet station it skirts the harbour on the right. Still active with commercial shipping up to 2500 tons, Watchet is the oldest port in the county and has recently celebrated its millenium. It was the prime reason for the railway, which arrived here in 1862, and the extension to Minehead took another 12 years to complete. It was in the docks at Watchet that Coleridge is believed to have found inspiration for *The Rime of the Ancient Mariner* in his conversations with sailors. Energetic passengers equipped for walking can leave the train here, or at the next station, Washford, to explore the remains of the West Somerset Mineral Railway. This fascinating line was built primarily to convey iron ore extracted from the Brendon Hills to Watchet harbour for shipment across the Bristol Channel to the foundries of south Wales. The most interesting part is the section from Comberow,

where an inclined plane ascended the slope of the hills.

Leaving Watchet the line turns inland and crosses the trackbed of the mineral railway before reaching Washford, where there is a small museum commemorating the Somerset & Dorset Railway, a route which once ran through the Mendips from Bath to Bournemouth. The line returns to the sea as it nears Blue Anchor, where the waiting room houses a museum of GWR artefacts. With marvellous views out to sea, the line hugs the shore to Dunster. A break in the 1-hour 20-minute journey to walk up the road to this attractive and interesting village is strongly recommended.

A long straight takes the railway past the largest holiday centre in the country and into the terminus and headquarters of the railway, where locomotives and carriages are repaired. Old Minehead and the 17th-century harbour are both the stuff of picture postcards.

Train service: most days between Easter and October, daily from June–September. Tel: 01643 707650/ 704996.

The signal box at Washford

BLUEBELL RAILWAY
East Sussex

SHEFFIELD PARK, 15 MILES (24 KM) NORTH-EAST OF BRIGHTON

*I*t is little wonder that the Bluebell Railway is probably the best-known preserved railway in Britain. Re-opened in 1960, it is the oldest of the former British Railways lines to be saved by preservationists – and one of its engines, *Stepney*, was used as the basis of an engine character by the Reverend W Awdry in his perennially popular children's books. Even those who have not heard of the Bluebell may recognise its southern terminus, since it takes its name from the nearby National Trust garden of Sheffield Park.

It is worth spending some time at Sheffield Park, admiring the superbly overhauled and repainted locomotives turned out by the well-equipped workshops, and looking at the small museum and model railway on the platform opposite the entrance. The

Crew taking a breather at Horsted Keynes

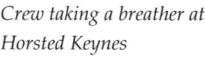

location of the signal box on the platform allows visitors to appreciate the burnished brass instruments and steel levers at closer quarters than most preserved railways.

Having been first in the field, the Bluebell was at a great advantage when it came to buying both locomotives and carriages from British Rail.

Steam traction still had eight years to run on Britain's national railways so there were over 10,000 locomotives and hundreds of different classes from which to choose. No railway can rival the Bluebell for the variety and antiquity of its coaches – many date from before World War I and few were built after the second. To sit in a beautifully upholstered compartment, surrounded by polished wood, ornate brass fittings and prints of rail destinations is one of the particular pleasures of a journey on the line.

Another hallmark of the Bluebell is attention to detail when it comes to authenticity, for few railways have been as meticulous in the way stations or rolling stock have been restored. The correct colours are scrupulously applied, and a journey from Sheffield Park takes passengers on something of a trip through time: this station has been renovated in the style of the London Brighton & South Coast Railway which built the line, opening in 1882; Horsted Keynes exemplifies a Southern Railway country junction of the 1930s; and the northern terminus at Kingscote, re-opened in 1994 as part of the drive to rejoin the main line at East Grinstead, is being renovated in the style of the 1950s. The journey also takes passengers from the eastern hemisphere to the west, crossing the line of the Greenwich

South Eastern & Chatham Railway P class 0-6-0T No 323, Bluebell, *one of the line's oldest – and smallest – locomotives*

*Workmanlike No 847
waiting at Sheffield Park for
another passenger load*

Meridian as it leaves Sheffield Park.

The train accelerates past the elegant starting signal at Sheffield Park so that the locomotive can get to grips with the steep 2-mile (3km) climb up Freshfield Bank. The woods that follow give the railway its name, for in May they are a mass of bluebells, almost irridescent in dappled spring sunshine. It is hard to believe that this idyllic countryside was the centre of Britain's iron industry during the Middle Ages, but woods like those beside the line were the source of the charcoal upon which the industry depended.

A final climb through a cutting brings the train into the imposing four-platform station at Horsted Keynes. The size of the station – even equipped with a subway – is astonishing for so remote a location, but this was once the junction for a line to Haywards Heath that was still in use when the Bluebell began operations. The route of the line, which closed in 1963, can be seen going off behind the signal box on the left on the approach to the station. Apart from the country park, ideal for picnics or for children to let off steam, Horsted Keynes has the

Bluebell's carriage and wagon works and sheds, where the varied skills needed to maintain the stock are practised. It is also worth allowing time for a drink in the delightfully restored bar on the middle platform, which must have consoled many a weary traveller waiting for a connection.

Out of Horsted Keynes, another climb faces northbound trains as they approach Sharpthorne Tunnel, at 780yds (714m) the longest tunnel on any preserved railway. The pictures of Kingscote station before a team began work following its purchase in 1985 are a good indication of what dedicated volunteers can achieve. An entire platform had to be replaced, and the filled-in subway cleared out – quite

apart from the eradication of both wet and dry rot in the station building.

Visitors to the Bluebell from the London area can take advantage of a bus service that runs non-stop from East Grinstead station to Kingscote, a ten-minute journey, every day that the railway operates and to coincide with the trains. Only visitors arriving at Kingscote by this bus are entitled to buy a ticket here, because of parking restrictions around the station. In a few years it should be possible to reach the Bluebell Railway by a simple cross-platform change at East Grinstead.

Train service: weekends throughout the year, but daily from May to September and on local school holidays. Tel: 01825 722370/723777.

Frequent routine checks are carried out when the trains are operating

ISLE OF WIGHT STEAM RAILWAY

Isle of Wight

SMALLBROOK JUNCTION, 1½ MILES (2.5 KM) SOUTH OF RYDE

Havenstreet station, a busy place with a museum about the island's railways as an added attraction

Queen Victoria popularised the Isle of Wight with her purchase of Osborne House and subsequent regular visits, and the island was once served by a characterful and extensive railway network. It was entirely worked by tank locomotives and, before the motor car eroded its traffic, carried huge numbers of holidaymakers.

The two lines that remain open could hardly be more different from each other, but they are linked by an interchange station, and the Ryde–Shanklin line, still part of the national railway system, is the best way to reach the Isle of Wight Steam Railway. First-time visitors from London to the island are often surprised by the train awaiting them as they step off the Wightlink ferry from Portsmouth at Ryde Pier – the last thing they would expect to see here is Piccadilly line stock. Much of it was over 30 years old when it was brought across the Solent in 1966, so it conveys something of a museum feel to what is an excellent service. From Ryde it is a short journey to Smallbrook Junction where in 1991 Network SouthEast built a new station to serve the preserved steam railway. Anyone who recalls the days of steam on *Vectis*, as the Romans called the island, would recognise most of the locomotives and carriages that run to Wooton, the western terminus of the 5-mile (8km) line.

It is one of the particular pleasures of the Isle of Wight Steam Railway that almost all its carriages were built before World War I, and the standard of restoration is quite exceptional. Often passengers spend the first mile or two of a journey admiring the interior of their carriage, rather than enjoying the scenery. The first part of the line, to the railway's headquarters at Havenstreet, is through woodland carpeted in bluebells in May followed by views across fields to distant hills.

It is well worth stopping off at Havenstreet to look at the museum about the island's railways, situated beside the shop in a former gasworks building. Rather surprising for a rural location, this structure was built as an act of benevolence by local landowner John Rylands, well-known to Mancunians for the library named after him. The engine shed can also be visited under supervision. The activity at Havenstreet today is a marked contrast to the peace of earlier times, when the tranquillity induced adders and a swan to find their way into the ground-level signal box – though not at the same time.

Train service: March to May and October, Thursday and Sunday; end May to end September, daily. Tel: 01983 882204/884343.

Still going strong – London Brighton & South Coast Railway 0-6-0T No 11 was built in 1878, one of the famous 'Terrier' AIX class

Narrow Gauge Railways

✳

*B*ritain had fewer public narrow gauge railways than any other country in Europe, so many of those that are open to tourists today carried no other passengers than the workmen connected with the industry for which the railway had been built. Almost every kind of mineral traffic spawned narrow gauge lines, and such railways were even built for sugar beet and potatoes. The 2ft 6in (762mm) gauge Sittingbourne & Kemsley Light Railway was built in 1906 to carry pulp and finished products between a dock on the River Swale and the huge paper mill at Sittingbourne, in Kent. Today some of the line's original locomotives haul passengers along the route. In other cases, a railway has been laid in an appropriate setting to illustrate past practice. At Amberley Chalk Pits Museum, near Arundel, a 2ft (610mm) gauge line has been laid on the 36-acre (14.5ha) site to carry visitors in authentic workmen's vehicles by a variety of steam and diesel locomotives.

Another line that never carried passengers was the Leighton Buzzard

Helen Kathryn *at Alston,*
South Tynedale Railway

Railway, in Bedfordshire, which connected sand quarries with the nearest standard gauge branch line. Its collection of locomotives includes a vertical-boilered de Winton, looking rather like an oversized tea urn on wheels, and an engine that spent its life at a pumping station in Calcutta. The firm ride of the home-built carriages is part of the experience.

Some narrow gauge lines have been built on the trackbed of a former standard gauge railway. The Teifi Valley Railway at Llandysul is a 2ft (610mm) gauge line that is built on the bed of the branch to Newcastle Emlyn at Henllan station. A Welsh quarry tank engine of 1894 provides the steam power. The picturesque standard gauge branch line that ran from England's highest market

town of Alston to a junction on the Newcastle–Carlisle line provides the basis of the South Tynedale Railway. Also of 2ft (610mm) gauge, it runs for 2 miles (3km) with locomotives from Natal, Poland, Spain and Turkey.

The Groudle Glen Railway on the Isle of Man is a reconstruction of the 2ft (610mm) line that ran in a spectacular cliff-top location to a menagerie. It even has one of the original locomotives – a Hunslet tank engine of 1896.

Most country houses, gardens or country parks choose a miniature gauge for a railway, but at Bicton Park, in Devon, the 18in (457mm) gauge was preferred for the Bicton Woodland Railway which takes visitors round the 18th-century park for almost 2 miles (3km). Its oldest steam locomotive, of 1916, once worked at Woolwich Arsenal.

The narrow gauge line is a popular additional attraction at the Amberley Chalk Pits Museum

KENT & EAST SUSSEX RAILWAY
Kent/East Sussex

TENTERDEN, 10 MILES (16 KM) SOUTH-WEST OF ASHFORD

*O*ne of the most extraordinary characters in the history of British railways was Lt Col Holman Frederick Stephens. After studying civil engineering at London University, he went on to build some very marginal railways, providing links that the large railway companies had declined to construct. One of these was the Kent & East Sussex Railway, originally running from Robertsbridge to Headcorn via the Cinque Port of Tenterden. Another now preserved

Getting ready to fill up with water at Northiam station

line with which he was involved as civil and mechanical engineer was the Ffestiniog Railway. None of his railways made more than slender profits and most lost money – a situation that was not allowed to continue for long after his death in 1931. The majority were gradually closed, but a goods service survived between Robertsbridge and Tenterden until 1961. A preservation bid was eventually successful after a court battle with the then Minister of Transport, and the

first section re-opened in 1974. Today some 7 miles (11.2 km) are operating, between Tenterden Town and Northiam, though the intention is to extend this for the 3½ miles (5.5 km) to Bodiam, to carry passengers to the National Trust's magnificent 14th-century castle, followed by the final 3 miles (5 km) to Robertsbridge and a link with the main Railtrack line.

Colonel Stephens's lines differed in character, but they had one thing in common – everything was done on a shoestring, including the engineering works and buildings, which were executed to the minimum standards or size possible. Most of the original buildings had been swept away by the time the preservationists took over, but a few remain, most notably the

station buildings at Tenterden where most passengers begin their journey. Indeed this was the only brick station building on the line, the others being of wood or corrugated iron. The adaptation of old buildings for the needs of visitors at Tenterden has been so well done that you would think the signal box had been opposite the station since the line opened in 1903; it was, in fact, rescued from Chilham between Ashford and Canterbury. The buffet is thought to be the oldest bus station in the country, possibly the oldest in the world, having been built in 1921 to serve Maidstone.

One of the pleasures of a journey on this line is its authentic collection of locomotives: one of the railway's two well-known 'Terrier' class locomotives

At present services operate between Tenterden and Northiam, but there plans to extend the line

Tenterden Town (above and right), the line's main station, lies just off the village high street

under the English Channel. The willows were planted during the 1930s in a rather sad gesture to augment the railway's meagre income.

The station at Wittersham Road may look all of a piece to anyone unversed in the nice distinctions of railway architecture, but the ensemble could hardly be more cosmopolitan. The station building came from north Wales, the water tower from Shrewsbury, the signals from Ireland actually worked on the railway during Colonel Stephens's years. Another diminutive tank engine, No 1556, was hired to the Kent & East Sussex during the 1930s and '40s. The railway's carriages are as heterogeneous a collection as might have been found on any of the Colonel's railways. Pride of place goes to the well-restored Victorian coaches, which range from rather spartan four-wheelers to the unique London & North Western Railway directors' saloon and a pair of family saloons.

The 50-minute journey from Tenterden takes you steeply downhill through pasture and woods to Rolvenden, where the engine shed and workshops have been situated since Colonel Stephens's day. Here the tank locomotives and one tender engine are restored and maintained. Passing beside willow- and reed-fringed channels on the right, the train skirts a freshwater crayfish farm and heads out across flat fields that were once and the signal box and lamps from Kent. The use of the word 'Road' was a kind of code that the railway companies used to indicate that the station was some distance from the village it purported to serve – in this case 3 miles (5km). However, the village with its windmill, oasthouse and even a Sir Edwin Lutyens' house, is well worth the walk.

The steep gradient that starts from the signal box at the platform end has the locomotive barking loudly through the cutting to the summit, after which a gentle curve leads on to the longest straight on the line as it crosses the Rother Levels to Northiam, with its beautifully restored station – a corrugated-iron original.

Train service: from March to October, ranging from Sundays only in March, to daily during June to August. Santa specials. Tel: 01580 762943.

MID-HANTS RAILWAY
Hampshire

ALRESFORD, 7 MILES (11.5 KM) EAST OF WINCHESTER

*T*ake the train from London Waterloo and you can be sitting in a train of the Mid-Hants Railway in little over an hour, simply by walking across the platform at Alton station. This easy interchange and the entry of the Mid-Hants into the town marked the culmination of over ten years' hard work by the preservation society formed in 1973 to re-open what had been known locally as the Watercress Line. The objective was to save the 10 miles (16km) between Alton and the largely Georgian market town of Alresford.

The line opened originally in 1865, joining Alton and the county town of Winchester. It had an unremarkable life, except during the two world wars: in the first it was busy with traffic from Aldershot to Southampton Docks, being the shortest route between the two; and during the second the district around Alresford was briefly home to the 47th Infantry Regiment, 9th Division US Army. During the build-up to D-Day, the newly built Winchester bypass became a tank park, and many tanks were unloaded at Alresford station.

The line saw occasional surges of traffic when it was used as a diversionary route while engineering work took place on the Waterloo–Southampton main line. For this purpose, the London & South Western Railway, which soon took over the independent company that built the line, had insisted it be built to main line standards. This was to prove a great boon to the Mid-Hants Railway, for one of the problems encountered by some preserved railways is that a branch line ancestry usually prevents the use of heavy

The Watercress Line (below) once again connects Alton to Alresford via Ropley (opposite)

locomotives. To cope with the often unprecedented passenger figures, many short trains have to be run with small engines, or the railway has to upgrade structures to accept heavier locomotives.

Otherwise this line's claim to fame was a pre-eminence in the dispatch of watercress. The pure chalk-spring waters of the River Arle long ago fostered this industry, which continues today. For almost a century the freshly gathered cress was packed into large wicker baskets, loaded at Alresford station into ventilated vans and sent up to London markets – a tradition which is perpetuated by the sale of watercress on Mid-Hants trains.

The railway survived a series of closure threats but finally succumbed in 1973. It was re-opened in stages between 1977 and 1985, the intention being to portray the character of a former London & South Western/ Southern Railway branch line. Each station is restored to represent a different era in the railway's history.

Leaving from platform three at Alton, trains pass the newly positioned signal box on the right and soon reach the site of Butts Junction where two other lines once led off, one to Fareham and the other to Basingstoke. The latter achieved lasting fame through its use for the filming of two railway classics: *The Wrecker* (1929) and *Oh! Mr Porter* (1937). The obvious exertions at the front end are explained by the gradient of 1 in 60 up to the first station at Medstead & Four Marks; coupled with the almost equally steep descent from there to Alresford, drivers referred to

Alresford station. The pretty Georgian town is a pleasant place to while away an hour

taking trains 'over the Alps'.

To the south, soon after passing the site of Butts Junction, lies the village of Chawton where the novelist Jane Austen lived for eight years – her house is now a museum. The station buildings at Medstead & Four Marks are more modest than those at the other stations, simply because the stationmaster's house was built as a separate structure rather than incorporated in the platform building. A vintage bus museum has been set up here, encouraging many to break their journey.

However, the most popular place to stop off is the other intermediate station, Ropley, for it is here that the Mid-Hants has its engine shed and workshops. There is also a picnic area with playground facilities on an

embankment, providing a grandstand view of the shed yard and departures on the main line. A Ropley Trail is being set up to incorporate local natural history as well as the railway aspects of the place. Most obvious to passengers is the ornate topiary on the platform, which continues a tradition started many decades ago. As the train drops down to Alresford, evidence of the watercress industry can be seen before the line enters a steep-sided chalk cutting on the approach to the southern terminus.

Train service: from March to October, daily in July and August, most days in June, weekends only other months. Santa specials. Tel: 01962 734866/733810.

BR 2-6-0 No 76017 leaving Medstead & Four Marks, one of the line's four public stations

A WALK AT FRIMLEY GREEN

*F*rimley Green is 3½ miles (5km) south of Camberley on the A321. The walk starts from Frimley Lodge Park, next to the church. For the parking area, drive into the park, bear right and follow the signs 'Canal South & Trim Trail'; the parking area is by the miniature railway.

From Frimley Lodge Park the walk goes along the canal then through woodland of pine and silver birch on sandy paths. Look out for grey squirrels, and woodland birds can be seen among the pine trees throughout the year; fungi, such as the colourful but poisonous fly agaric, abound in autumn. There are pike in the canal, where moorhens can usually be seen.

The miniature railway at Frimley Lodge Park

The walk is about 1½ miles (2.4km) long, and level, easy walking, with one short flight of fairly steep wooden steps. Seats along the canal offer places to pause, and the nearby King's Head pub has a garden and play area for children.

🐕🐕🐕🐕

DIRECTIONS

From the car park walk a few yards up the track to the canal. Turn right onto the towpath and continue for about ¾ mile (1.2km) to the road bridge. Go up the steps and turn left across the bridge. Opposite Potters pub, turn left along a track and bear right along the signposted bridleway. Almost immediately bear left off the main path along a narrow footpath.

Continue through the pine woods at the back of a school, keeping to the left wherever there is a choice. On reaching the marked bridleway turn left and keep left at the next signpost. Remain on this path for about ¾ mile and eventually emerge on to Windmill Lane.

Continue ahead to the road, turn left and after a few yards cross the narrow bridge over the canal (with care – there is no pavement). A few yards ahead is the King's Head pub. Take the path to the left, immediately after the bridge, leading back down to the canal towpath. Turn right and return along the canal to the car park.

Frimley Lodge Park

Covering nearly 70 acres (28ha) of meadowland and mature woodland, Frimley Lodge Park includes formal

The Basingstoke Canal, built in the late 18th century to link Basingstoke and London

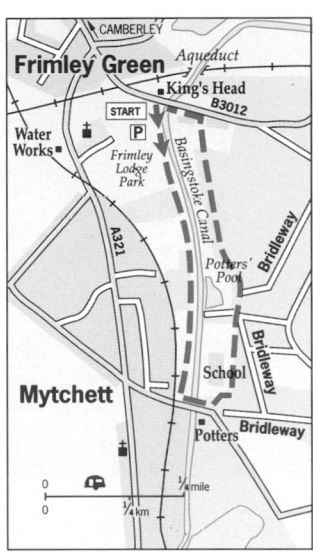

play areas, picnic sites with barbecue facilities, a trim trail, a miniature railway (which operates on selected Sunday afternoons), a pitch and putt course and a pavilion with a cafeteria.

The Canal

Built between 1789 and 1794, the Basingstoke Canal was once busy with barges carrying timber for ship- and house-building, grain, malt and other produce from north Hampshire to London, returning with cargoes of coal and manufactured goods. It was formally re-opened in 1991 by HRH The Duke of Kent after a long programme of restoration begun in 1974.

The canal is stocked with fish, and day fishing tickets can be purchased at all local tackle shops. They must be obtained in advance.

In the sheds at New Romney station, the railway's headquarters

---
✤
ROMNEY, HYTHE & DYMCHURCH RAILWAY
Kent

HYTHE, 4½ MILES (7.5 KM) SOUTH OF FOLKESTONE

✤

Miniature railways have a fascination of their own, not least for children, witnessed by the enduring popularity of the Romney, Hythe & Dymchurch Railway since it opened in 1927. Although the number of miniature railways has mushroomed since World War II, the concept of the Romney, Hythe and Dymchurch remains unique. The reason for this is largely due to its creator, Captain Jack Howey, who had the wealth to build a main line railway in miniature, with double track, substantial stations and powerful locomotives capable of a scale speed of 75mph (120kph).

A strong commercial case for such lavishness would be hard to make – no miniature railway of comparable length has been able to justify more than a single line, for example. But with the rental income from a good chunk of central Melbourne in

Australia, Captain Howey did not have to worry about sceptical bank managers. To power his trains, Howey ordered nine steam locomotives, five based on the elegant Pacific design by Sir Nigel Gresley for the London & North Eastern Railway, two freight types for aggregate traffic that never materialised and a pair of Canadian-style Pacifics – Howey particularly enjoyed his railway holidays there.

The Duke of York, later King George VI, drove the first train into New Romney and the railway soon became well known as the World's Smallest Public Railway. It flourished during the 1930s and played its part in the defence of the Kent coast when an armoured train was built, sporting a couple of machine guns and an anti-tank rifle. Powered by a protected 4-8-2, *Samson*, it made regular forays from its dummy hill near Dymchurch.

Some economies were made on the railway as the popularity of holidays abroad eroded its traffic during the 1960s, but new management following Howey's death has helped to revive the railway's fortunes, and it remains one of the finest miniature railways in the world. Amongst many innovations is an observation car equipped with licensed bar. As well as being a tourist attraction, the Romney, Hythe & Dymchurch has a practical role in the community: since 1977 it has carried about 200 children a day from the Dymchurch area to and from school in New Romney.

Hythe is the largest resort on the line, with some fine Victorian hotels, and the terminal station still has the only original overall roof spanning its three platforms. It stands beside the Royal Military Canal, built to deter invasion by Napoleon. The station's size, coupled with the water tower, signal box, turntable and engine shed

The locomotive No 8, Hurricane (below) was temporarily renamed in 1994 after accidental damage

(now disused) help to create a main line atmosphere. As the long train gathers pace under the signal gantry at the platform end, the line is fringed by back gardens on one side and the remains of the canal on the other. The pace quickens as the line enters open country with wide views over the flat land of Romney Marsh, renowned for smuggling activities following the decline of the Cinque ports. In the distance can be seen the gently rising hills of Lympne, with its extraordinary castle built for Sir Philip Sassoon.

Bowling along the flat land towards Dymchurch at about 25mph (40kph), the clickety-clack of the rail joints provides a sound almost consigned to history on all but secondary routes on modern railways. After one of the line's many level crossings, the train reaches Dungeness, which once had an overall roof, signal box and sidings. On the approach to the next station at Jefferstone Lane, look out for the bungalow in which E Nesbit spent the last years of her life, having achieved fame with *The Railway Children*; it is on the left as you enter the station and is named 'The Long Boat'.

Open fields, a shallow cutting and a tunnel under a main road precede the railway's headquarters at New Romney. Apart from the attraction of watching engines coming off shed or shunting carriages, the station has a popular model exhibition with show-case models and two impressive model railways. Although the station has a huge new roof spanning the running lines, elements of Howey's original station survive, including the wooden clock tower.

Wartime damage to the line between New Romney and Dungeness wrecked the track so badly that the second line was never replaced. Now trains can cross at one point, Romney Sands, on

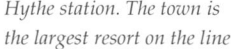

Hythe station. The town is the largest resort on the line

New Romney, where there are model railways and a model exhibition

this section of the line that traverses one of the most unusual areas of Britain. For part of the way the line is fringed by single-storey bungalows at Greatstone, most of them built during the 1930s and many still retaining the architectural character of that decade.

The broad expanse of shingle that surrounds the two nuclear power stations and two lighthouses at Dungeness is for some an alienating and barren landscape. But for anyone with an interest in natural history, it offers a diverse selection of rare plants with colonies of moths and butterflies, and is a sanctuary for birds. Having reached the end of the line, the 1904 lighthouse is a good reason to delay the return to New Romney, with a rewarding panorama from the top.

Train service: daily from April to September and October half-term; weekends in March and first half of October. Tel: 01797 363256/362353.

THE BATTLEFIELD LINE
Leicestershire

SHACKERSTONE, 5 MILES (8KM) NORTH-WEST OF MARKET BOSWORTH

*B*osworth Field is the battlefield in question, the place where in 1485 Richard III was defeated and killed and Henry VII became the first Tudor king of England. The name given to the 4¾-mile (7.5km) line reflects the importance to the railway of that historic site, but the Battlefield Trail and Visitor Centre are not the only attractions for visitors to the railway.

Parallel to the approach road to Shackerstone station, where most passengers begin their journey, is the Ashby Canal on which barges began their trade in 1804. This, like the later railway which opened in 1873, was built to improve communications with the coalfield around Ashby and Moira. Leisure boats now use the canal, and the towpath makes for a pleasant walk as it keeps company with the railway to the south.

Schoolchildren make up a good proportion of the railway's passengers, since few 'educational resources' can offer teachers the combination of a dynastic war and the age of steam. Shackerstone station museum displays an impressive if rather bewildering

Lamps and other signalling equipment are among the railway paraphernalia on display at Shackerstone station museum

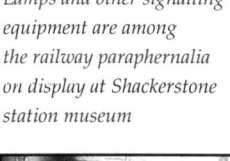

array of railway artefacts, including a telephone earpiece that tells railway tales, and visitors can soon understand the rudiments of signalling as well as pull levers. Every effort has been made to re-create the character of the country railway and portray its importance to the community, which witnessed the arrival of Edward VII in 1906 when he visited nearby Gopshall Hall (now demolished).

Only industrial locomotives are based permanently on the railway, so more powerful engines on loan from other railways or museums can often be seen at work. The gently undulating Leicestershire landscape rarely affords wide panoramas but the railway embankment gives something of a grandstand view as pheasants brazenly strut the neighbouring fields.

It is worth alighting at the one intermediate station, Market Bosworth, to explore the pretty town where Samuel Johnson once taught at the grammar school. At journey's end the terminus beside the battlefield is served by the attractive station building from Leicester Humberstone

Road, which was dismantled and skilfully re-erected. A path from the station leads to the trail around the battlefield, with information boards which take you back to that August day when the course of British history was decisively changed.

Train service: Saturdays, Sundays and Bank Holiday Mondays, from Easter to October; also diesel service Wednesdays, July and August. Santa specials. Tel: 01827 880754.

1994 saw the Shackerstone Railway Society's silver jubilee

With its headquarters at Aylsham, the BVR runs over the old Great Eastern Wroxham–Aylsham line

BURE VALLEY RAILWAY
Norfolk

WROXHAM, 7 MILES (11 KM) NORTH-EAST OF NORWICH

When the writer and broadcaster Miles Kington opened the Bure Valley Railway in 1990, it marked the completion of the longest miniature railway to be built in Britain since the 1920s. The 9-mile (14.5km) line links the 'capital' of the Norfolk Broads at Wroxham with the town of Aylsham, where the market square is ringed with fine 18th-century houses, and it serves a local transport function as well as being a tourist attraction. Conveniently, the main line and Bure Valley stations at Wroxham are connected by a footbridge, and the town centre at Aylsham is only a short walk from the station.

The 15in (375mm) gauge railway is built on the trackbed of a Great Eastern Railway branch line that left the Norwich to Cromer line at Wroxham and meandered through gently rolling country to join the Dereham–Wells line at the isolated junction of County School. Although the line was open for freight until the early 1980s, 17 bridges had to be repaired, a ¼-mile (0.5km) tunnel built under the Aylsham bypass and 6000 tons of crushed shingle brought in to replace the ballast.

The journey in the comfortable carriages takes visitors past the walls of the Elizabethan Little Hautbois Hall, its blocked-up windows still recalling the aesthetic damage done by the

window tax, which was in force from 1695 to 1851. Heading for Aylsham, the train soon runs parallel to the River Bure, where swans can sometimes be seen in majestic flight and geese are ten a penny. The village of Buxton with Lammas, the two separated by the Bure, is served by a station on the line and an interesting place to break the journey. The attractive Church of St Andrew can be glimpsed from the train, but the Quaker Burial Ground and resting place of the author of *Black Beauty*, Anna Sewell, has to be sought out.

After rattling through the tunnel into Aylsham station, the train draws to a halt under a huge overall roof, a very grand terminus for a railway of this small gauge. The engine shed beside the station gives visitors the opportunity to admire the fine collection of surprisingly powerful locomotives, the most recent additions being based on an Indian Railways' narrow gauge design. Keen walkers can use their legs in either direction, since the line runs alongside the Bure Valley Walk; this path connects with a network of paths from Norwich and North Walsham created by Broadland District Council. Guides to the routes are available.

Train service: most days from Easter to end September; October half-term holidays. Santa specials. Tel: 01263 733858.

Winson 2-6-2 No 6, built in 1994, is the newest ocomotive in service on the line

FOXFIELD STEAM RAILWAY
Staffordshire

BLYTHE BRIDGE, 6 MILES (9.5 KM) SOUTH-EAST OF STOKE-ON-TRENT

Opposite: on the Foxfield line – a surprisingly rural and scenic route for a former colliery railway

A former colliery railway in the heart of the Staffordshire coalfield might seem to appeal to none but the most avid enthusiast, but don't be put off – the views from these trains are a far cry from bleak post-industrial landscapes. The spoil tips from the colliery are now largely overgrown, and for most of the journey the line passes through woods that threaten to engulf the train, so close do the branches come, or past fields of grazing cows or corn. In the distance the fringes of the Staffordshire moors can be seen, and across the valley is the village after which the line named its northern terminus, Dilhorne. It is denoted by the octagonal spire of All Saints' church.

Until the number of British coal mines was decimated, most collieries were connected to the railway system by sidings or by a branch line. Most of these have been built over or returned to nature, but close to Blythe Bridge station on the Stoke–Derby line is a surviving branch that served a mine in the once prosperous Staffordshire coalfield. Coal was mined at Foxfield in the 17th century, but it was 1893 before a branch was built off the North Staffordshire Railway, known locally as the 'Knotty' after the county emblem it adopted. The mine closed in 1965 but a 2¾-mile (4.5km) section was saved by a group of enthusiasts. The final part to the mine itself did not become part of the Foxfield Light Railway, and this is a great shame because it had the steepest gradient and the mine buildings could have formed an interesting feature.

This loss prompted the group to establish a new station, engine shed and museum at the opposite end of the line close to Blythe Bridge. Visitors usually have a look round the collection of locomotives before taking a ride – all are tank engines and were once employed in industrial use, some of them in the Midland counties. Perhaps most surprising on a former colliery railway is the provision of a bar and observation car, known as the Bass Belle, which provides welcome refreshment and helps the railway's coffers.

The small size of most of the Foxfield's locomotives means that they have to work hard pulling the former British Railways carriages, but try to visit on one of the special days, when there is a demonstration of coal wagons being worked up the 1 in 25 gradient from the colliery. These demonstrations provide a spectacle and sound that are unforgettable.

Train service: from Easter to September, Sundays and Bank Holiday weekends. Santa specials. Tel: 01782 396210.

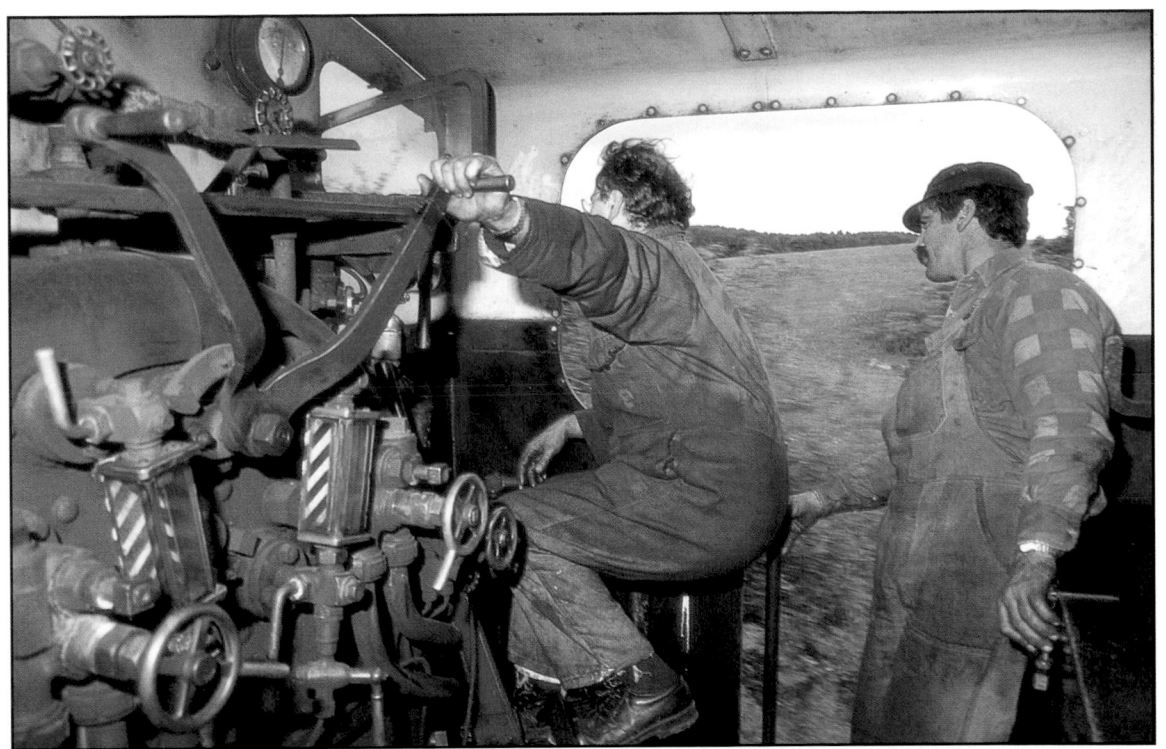

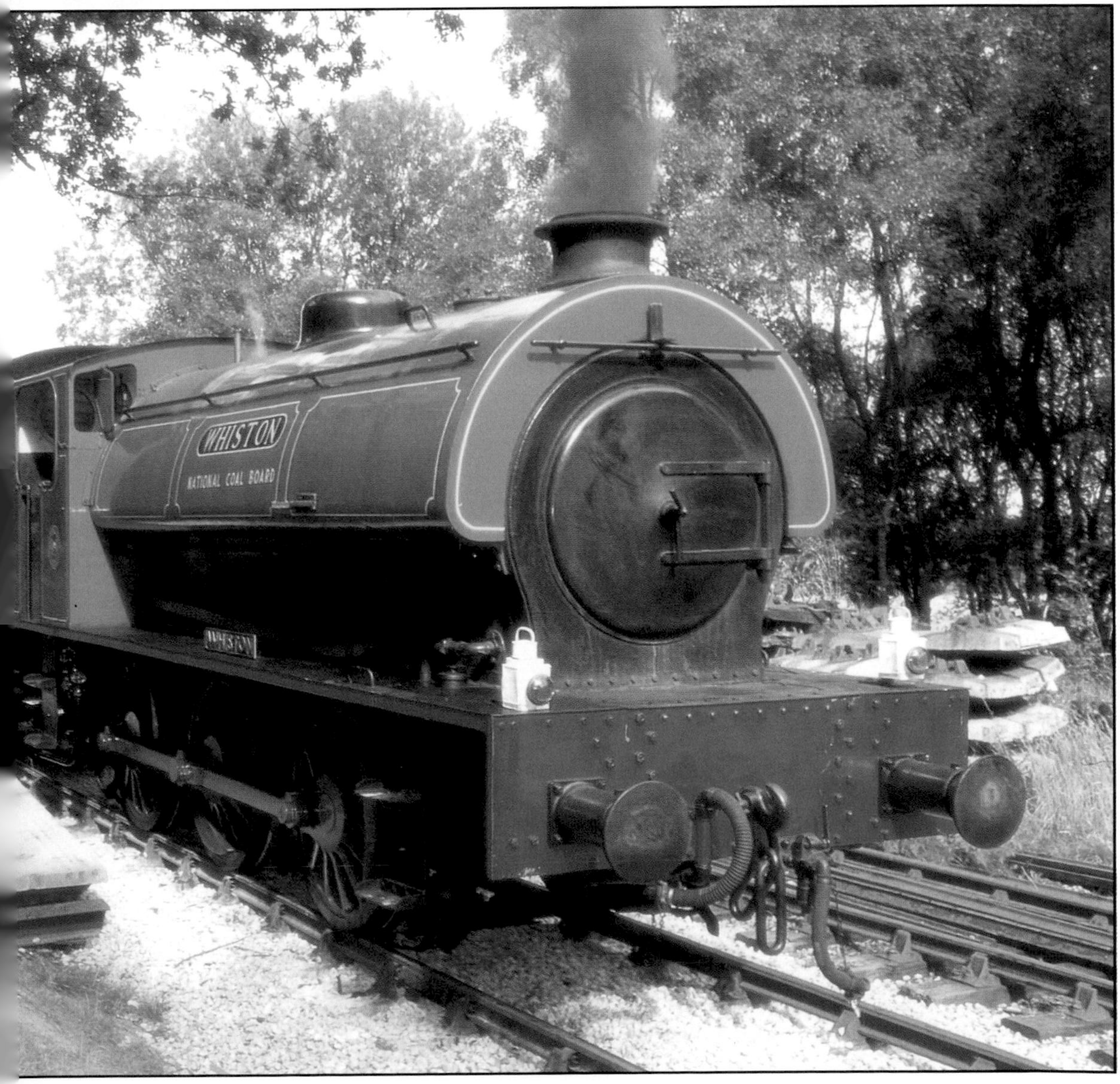
WHISTON
NATIONAL COAL BOARD
WHISTON

GREAT CENTRAL RAILWAY
Leicestershire

LOUGHBOROUGH, 9 MILES (14.5 KM) NORTH OF LEICESTER

With so many preserved railways in Britain, it is difficult to offer visitors something unique, but the Great Central Railway succeeds as the only line to re-create the atmosphere of the main line railway complete with double track and goods loops for expresses to overtake slower trains. The line is well placed to do this, since the route was once part of Britain's last great main line, the Great Central Railway, which ran from just north of Nottingham to a new London terminus at Marylebone. It was intended by its visionary chairman, Sir Edward Watkin, to become part of a continuous railway from the north of England to France, through a tunnel under the English Channel which was to be built

Loughborough station, the largest in preservation

by an associated company. Today's Great Central serves as a reminder of that superbly engineered line, most of which was closed during the 1960s.

The starting point for most passengers is Loughborough, where the station is the largest in preservation. Film companies often take advantage of its size, emphasised by the long, ornate canopy along the island platform; the station was recently used for the filming of *Shadowlands*, starring Anthony Hopkins. Before boarding a train, passengers are invited to inspect the impressive workshops and engine shed, which can be reached by a footpath to the north of the station. The original signal box that still controls train movements at the station stands beside the path, and visitors are normally welcomed by the signalman. There is also a museum in part of the old lift shaft for luggage, which gives visitors a good idea of the history of the railway on which they are about to travel.

As befits a main line railway, the Great Central has some large steam locomotives amongst its fleet of 23, and it frequently has visiting engines to add variety. Leaving Loughborough for the half-hour journey, you are soon in lovely countryside, often with woods on the horizon as a backdrop to the gently undulating landscape.

The first station, at Quorn & Woodhouse, has a picnic site adjacent to the typical island platform

Stoking the firebox

arrangment, in which tracks pass either side of a single platform. Shortly beyond Quorn is the scenic highlight of the journey as the train crosses Swithland Reservoir on a long viaduct. Now a sanctuary for birds, the reservoir had to be drained for the construction of the viaduct. At Swithland Sidings the Great Central Railway's impressive work to restore the look of the old main line can be best appreciated, though there is no station here. The goods loops have been installed here and double-tracking south to Rothley is underway. You may also see a goods train of seemingly endless coal wagons pass by, for another Great Central project is

Watering time again

the re-creation of the 'Windcutter' fast coal trains which once used the line. To achieve this, a large number of 16-ton mineral wagons has been assembled.

Try to find time to break your journey at Rothley, for it is a delightful station with one of the best preserved rooms – the humble, but superbly refurbished parcels office. The station is gaslit and has been restored using the colours of the old Great Central Railway. The signal box was rescued from Wembley in London to replace the original, long since demolished; its most notorious inhabitant was a signalman with a penchant for nude bathing in the station watertrough. The large shed to the east of the line is the railway's carriage shed and works.

Leaving Rothley, look out for Rothley Brook which was used as a canal in Roman times. Just beyond the site of Belgrave & Birstall station, demolished in 1977, is the Great Central's new southern terminus. This promises to be one of the most ambitious ever projects in railway preservation, for the intention is to build a three-platform station with a two-storey building based on Marylebone. A new engine shed, turntable and museum will be provided, with events lawn and adjacent nature reserve.

One day the Great Central may operate trains to the outskirts of Nottingham, for at the country park at Ruddington an affiliated group is creating a northern base from which it is hoped to lay track to the south. This would double the present run of 7½ miles (12km).

Train service: weekends all year, weekdays from June to September. Santa specials. Tel: 01509 230726.

London & North East Railway s No 1306, the Mayflower

Working Museums

*A*lthough visitors to the four principal operating museums would find them comparable, they each began in very different circumstances. The Great Western Society exists to preserve anything to do with that railway company – 'God's Wonderful Railway' as it has long been called, either with reverence or derision depending upon the speaker's allegiance. The Society's search for a home for its locomotives, carriages and wagons ended at the former Great Western Railway locomotive depot at Didcot in Oxfordshire. Here the Great Western Society has developed the museum to embrace signal boxes, signalling, historic railway buildings and small relics, displayed in a setting softened by trees and enlivened by two demonstration lines for operating days.

The Birmingham Railway Museum was founded not only as an engine

shed for a growing collection of locomotives and carriages, but also as an engineering workshop to preserve the specialised machine tools developed to maintain the steam locomotive. With the end of steam on British railways these were being discarded as rapidly as the locomotives themselves. Visitors can see something of the heavy engineering work that goes on here from the gallery above the workshop area. There is also a museum, a signal box to control the demonstration line and a turntable display area.

Steamtown at Carnforth, in Cumbria, is very similar to the Birmingham Railway Museum, the principal difference being that the old steam shed at Carnforth was taken over largely intact, whereas the Birmingham museum has had to erect a new building. As a result, Steamtown has inherited something of the

Careful maintenance work in the original steam shed at Carnforth

atmosphere of the steam age, with the inspection and ash pits, water hydrants for boiler washouts, smoke ducts along the underside of the roof and smaller items like roster and notice boards. It too has a signal box as well as a miniature railway running the length of the long site. Like the Birmingham Railway Museum, Steamtown is often home to locomotives that are running excursions over BR lines.

Bressingham Steam Museum, at Diss in Norfolk, is largely the creation of Alan Bloom, a successful nurseryman with a passion for steam locomotives, and has no less than three different gauge railways. The 15in (375mm) and 2ft (610mm) gauge lines take visitors around the nursery, while the standard gauge runs down an avenue of trees – modest tank engines would not look out of place here, but many visitors are astonished to see an engine the size of the Britannia Pacific *Oliver Cromwell* giving rides over a few hundred yards of track. There is also a magnificent display of traction and fire engines, and many rare railway relics.

Above: in all, there are some 50 road and rail engines on display at Bressingham

Below: the engine sheds at Carnforth

MIDLAND RAILWAY CENTRE
Derbyshire

RIPLEY, 10 MILES (16 KM) NORTH OF DERBY

*T*he Midland Railway Trust is not just for railway buffs, though it does have an excellent working line of 3½ miles (5km) with three stations along the way. One of these stations also has a large museum, a farm park with lots of animals, a country park and a narrow gauge railway. Tourist railways are increasingly trying to expand their range of activities or points of interest to broaden their appeal and in this respect the Midland Railway Centre has succeeded admirably. The centre was something of a pioneer, starting off with a grandiose vision, and this was, in part, because it was the brainchild of local authorities who wanted to commemorate the railway which had had such an impact on the county town and its environs. Credit for the realisation of this bold plan, however, is due to the volunteer organisation formed to support the venture, since local government reorganisation ended the role of local authorities as the driving force.

The line itself is the remains of a

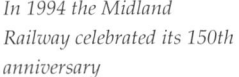
In 1994 the Midland Railway celebrated its 150th anniversary

Midland Railway branch that was built primarily for coal and goods traffic but also had a suburban service from Derby. At Hammersmith, the western terminus of the Centre, a line went off west to Ambergate. Its survival was largely due to the rail connection to the famous Butterley Company ironworks, set up in the 1790s – its most famous contract was the roof for St Pancras station in London, but it also exported widely, and ironwork for such stations as Buenos Aires was taken out by the Midland Railway for transfer to the docks.

A journey over this line begins at Butterley. There was nothing left of the original structures so the handsome station building was moved stone by stone from Whitwell in the north of the county. A model railway, buffet and shop help to pass the time before departure for Swanwick and Riddings Junction. The signal box at Butterley, one of four Midland Railway boxes on the line, was originally at the remote site of Ais Gill on the Settle & Carlisle railway.

Signal-changing: the railway has three working restored signal boxes and a fourth on display at the museum

The Centre's museum (best visited on the return journey from Riddicks Junction) is passed on the right as the train steams past Swanwick Junction. As the valley opens up, cottages beside the Cromford Canal can be seen, and on a hillside to the south is a monument to William Jessop, who both built the canal and helped to found the Butterley Company. At Riddick Junction the locomotive runs round the train before returning to Swanwick; in due course the line will be extended to a new station beside the Nottingham–Sheffield line.

The complex at Swanwick could take much of the day to see properly. It is dominated by the Matthew Kirtley Museum, named after a locomotive superintendent of the Midland who designed one of the locomotives in the museum. This huge building contains most of the Centre's stock and also functions as a repair shop for both steam and diesel engines. Behind the shed is an engineering workshop, to which access is limited, and beyond that a miniature railway. A road transport museum is under construction for the display of a collection ranging from early bicycles to double-decker buses. Past Johnson's Buffet (named after another Midland Railway locomotive superintendent) is Brittain Pit Farm Park, centred on a range of brick buildings, where a wide variety of animals can be seen at close quarters. Near the demonstration signal box, in

which a signalman illustrates the intricacies of the job, a narrow gauge railway takes visitors into the 35-acre (14ha) country park. Here a network of paths leads to a series of ponds, to the remains of Grumblethorpe Colliery and to the mouth of the Cromford Canal tunnel. This was blocked off in 1909 following an earlier collapse through subsidence. The canal was finally abandoned in 1944, although recent restoration of the Ambergate–Cromford section has returned boats to that part of the waterway.

An alternative to taking the train back from Swanwick Junction is to walk along the top of the cutting between there and Butterley. However, westbound trains run through Butterley without stopping, so if you plan to do this, make sure you purchase a ticket for unlimited travel, which applies on all but a few special days. Then you can catch an outward train again, and return the whole way by rail.

The last section of the line is one of the most photographed, crossing a long stone embankment across Butterley Reservoir; this structure was built in the 1930s to replace a bridge. At Hammersmith, the locomotive again runs round, under the control of a signal box rescued from Kilby Bridge, Leicester. Work is in progress here to create a small country station.

Train service: on 214 days during the year, Wednesdays and weekends. Tel: 01773 570140.

Right: getting ready for the off in traditional manner

Opposite: BR 2-6-4T No 80080, one of the 15 locomotives currently in service on the line

Black Prince ?

*Deutsche Bundesbahn class
52 2-10-0 No 7173 receives
a final check-over*

NENE VALLEY RAILWAY
Cambridgeshire

WANSFORD, 8 MILES (13 KM) WEST OF PETERBOROUGH

The Nene Valley Railway has been a major asset to feature film makers, since it is the only railway in Britain which has such an extensive overseas collection – locomotives and rolling stock from 11 different countries can be seen here. Well-known films whose 'foreign' railway sequences were shot on the Nene Valley line include *Octopussy*, with Roger Moore as James Bond, *The Dirty Dozen* and *Murder on the Orient Express.*

This diverse collection was acquired partly by accident but also through necessity. By the time moves were afoot in the early 1970s to preserve a stretch of the railway along the Nene Valley, the only available locomotives in Britain were those languishing in Barry scrapyard in south Wales. Having been exposed to salt air for years, they were a costly proposition to restore. Moreover, Peterborough Development Corporation, which had bought the line from British Rail,

wanted to see trains running quickly. An offer of a Swedish engine seemed to be the answer to the problem, not least because it was necessary to demolish only one overbridge to make the line useable by locomotives built to the larger continental loading gauge. The Nene Valley soon attracted other foreign engines, and visitors can see examples from France, Germany, Austria, Poland, Sweden and Denmark. The railway also has a good collection of British engines, if the propensity to stick all the plumbing outside the boiler is not to your taste.

This line is very good for children. It has a locomotive permanently called *Thomas*, named by the Reverend W Awdry himself, and young visitors particularly relish the tunnel. There is also the 2000-acre (800ha) Nene Park – an ideal place to break the journey, and served by the intermediate station at Ferry Meadows – which has play areas for children, a miniature railway, cycle

hire, nature trails and picnic sites.

Most passengers start their journey at the line's headquarters at Wansford, where you can also look round the engine shed. The original station building – an architectural gem in Jacobean style by the accomplished architect William Livock – is sadly not owned by the Nene Valley Railway, although their signal box is one of the finest on a preserved railway. Trains head west through the 671yd (614m) Wansford Tunnel to the site of Yarwell Junction, where the lines to Rugby and Northampton divided. Here trains reverse and head back through Wansford, cross the river and turn into the 3-mile (5km) straight to Ferry Meadows. Passing broad cornfields, followed by the man-made country park, the line terminates at Orton Mere in Peterborough, a short walk from the main line station.

Train service: Sundays from January to March, weekends from April to October, and a variable midweek service from June to August. Santa specials. Tel: 01780 784444.

Crowds eagerly await the arrival of Thomas

NORTH NORFOLK RAILWAY

SHERINGHAM, 4 MILES (6.5 KM) WEST OF CROMER

*T*he 25-minute journey on the North Norfolk Railway might be an eye-opener for those who think of Norfolk as a flat county. For much of the outward journey over the 5¼ miles (8.5km) from Sheringham to Holt, the locomotive has to work hard on gradients as steep as 1 in 80, but the open embankments enable passengers to enjoy the marvellous views over the sea to the north and the woods inland.

Once part of the Midland & Great Northern Railway, the section that forms today's North Norfolk Railway was built to cater as much for holiday traffic as to serve local communities, but the seasonal nature of the line's income led to its downfall. It closed in stages between 1959 and 1964, although a new station at Sheringham can still be reached by train from Norwich and it is only a few minutes' walk between the stations. Re-opened to passengers in 1975, the original

Lovely coastal views on the approach to Weybourne station

Sheringham station reflects the number of passengers it handled when named trains like the *Broadsman* and *Norfolkman* called here. The elaborate cast-iron brackets supporting the canopy are adorned with hanging baskets, and there is plenty to look at while waiting for the next train, including a museum portraying the history of the Midland & Great Northern Railway.

After viewing the delightful landscape on the way to Weybourne, passengers will not be surprised to learn that it has been designated an Area of Outstanding Natural Beauty. Once a golf course on the seaward side is left behind, the land on either side is attractive arable country with fields of barley, carrots and sugarbeet. Inland the fields rise up to the

woodlands of Sheringham Park, landscaped by Humphry Repton, and regarded by him as his finest work. It is also interesting to see the railway from the park, from a viewpoint which puts the trains into the perspective of a fine panorama of coastline and agricultural hinterland.

The one intermediate station, at Weybourne, offers several reasons to postpone the final leg of the journey to Holt. It is here that locomotives are restored, and guided tours can be arranged by the stationmaster. A board on the station suggests walks through nearby Kelling Woods, and in the opposite direction, a mile from the station, is the village of Weybourne. As well as the ruins of an Augustinian priory and windmill, walkers are close to Weybourne Hope where exceptionally deep water made it a likely place for an attempted invasion in 1588 and again during World War II. The section to Holt climbs across Kelling Heath with good views out to sea. Although the station at Holt is yet to be developed, passengers in high season are often met by a horse-bus for conveyance into the Georgian market town.

Train service: daily from April to September; weekends in March; Wednesday to Sunday in October; also February half-term and Santa specials. Tel: 01263 822045/825449.

Ring Haw *at Sheringham: the town also has a main line station with services to Norwich*

BALA LAKE RAILWAY
Gwynedd

LLANUWCHLLYN, 13 MILES (21 KM) NORTH OF DOLGELLAU

There is something special about railways that run alongside an expanse of water, and no tourist railway can rival the 1ft 11⅝in (600mm) gauge Bala Lake Railway, for it is seldom out of sight of its accompanying acres of water. Beyond are the peaks of the Aran Mountains, some rising to almost 3000ft (914m).

Most visitors begin their 25-minute journey at the southern terminus of Llanuwchllyn, because the temporary terminus outside Bala has limited facilities and access – a ¾-mile (1.2km) extension to a new station closer to the centre is planned. The station at Llanuwchllyn was once a crossing place on the single line standard gauge railway that linked the coast at Morfa Mawddach, beyond Dolgellau, with Corwen and Ruabon. This was closed by Dr Beeching in 1965, along with hundreds of miles of other Welsh railways.

Re-opened in stages from 1972, the Bala Lake Railway now runs for 4½ miles (7km) and is the best way to enjoy the scenery around the lake – the parallel road requires total concentration from drivers. Before boarding the train, it is worth having a look in the 1896 signal box, which still controls the points and signals and is often open to passengers. Trains are normally hauled by one of the three steam locomotives. Appropriately, two of them once worked in the Dinorwic slate quarries at Llanberis. As the railway joins the lake, a large house can be seen across the water: Glanllyn Hall was the Williams Wynne family home and is now an outdoor activities centre. Sir Watkin was a shareholder of the company that built the line, and when he disembarked at Glanllyn Halt a flag would be hoisted to summon his boat.

The line meanders beside the lake, the occasional headland seeming to take the railway inland. Anglers are often seen, some doubtless attracted by the lake's unique primitive species of fish, the gwyniad, which has been protected since 1988. A variety of walks from Llangower station entices some passengers to break their journey, while the historic market town of Bala is only ten minutes' walk from the terminus.

Train service: daily from April to September, though no Monday or Friday service except Bank Holidays and in July and August. Santa specials. Tel: 01678 540666.

Maid Marian *(left and below)* is one of three locomotives regularly in use on this very scenic line. Others are on display

BRECON MOUNTAIN RAILWAY

Powys

PANT, 2 MILES (3 KM) NORTH OF MERTHYR TYDFIL

Narrow gauge railways never found favour in Britain on the scale that they did in most other countries throughout the world. Only in north Wales was there a significant mileage. So it is not surprising that new narrow gauge tourist railways have had to look abroad for their motive power. The 1ft 11¾in (610mm) Brecon Mountain Railway is a good example: of its four steam locomotives, only one worked in Britain, two being bought from South Africa and one from the former East Germany.

The impressive railway headquarters are situated at Pant, to the north of Merthyr Tydfil, in an area that was an early cradle of industrial invention and enterprise. The legacy of this activity can still be seen during a journey on the Brecon Mountain Railway, which is largely built on the trackbed of the standard gauge line that once linked Merthyr Tydfil to Brecon. A ramp takes visitors up from the car park and booking office to platform level, where the well-equipped workshops and repair work on locomotives can be viewed from a gallery.

The most used locomotive is the

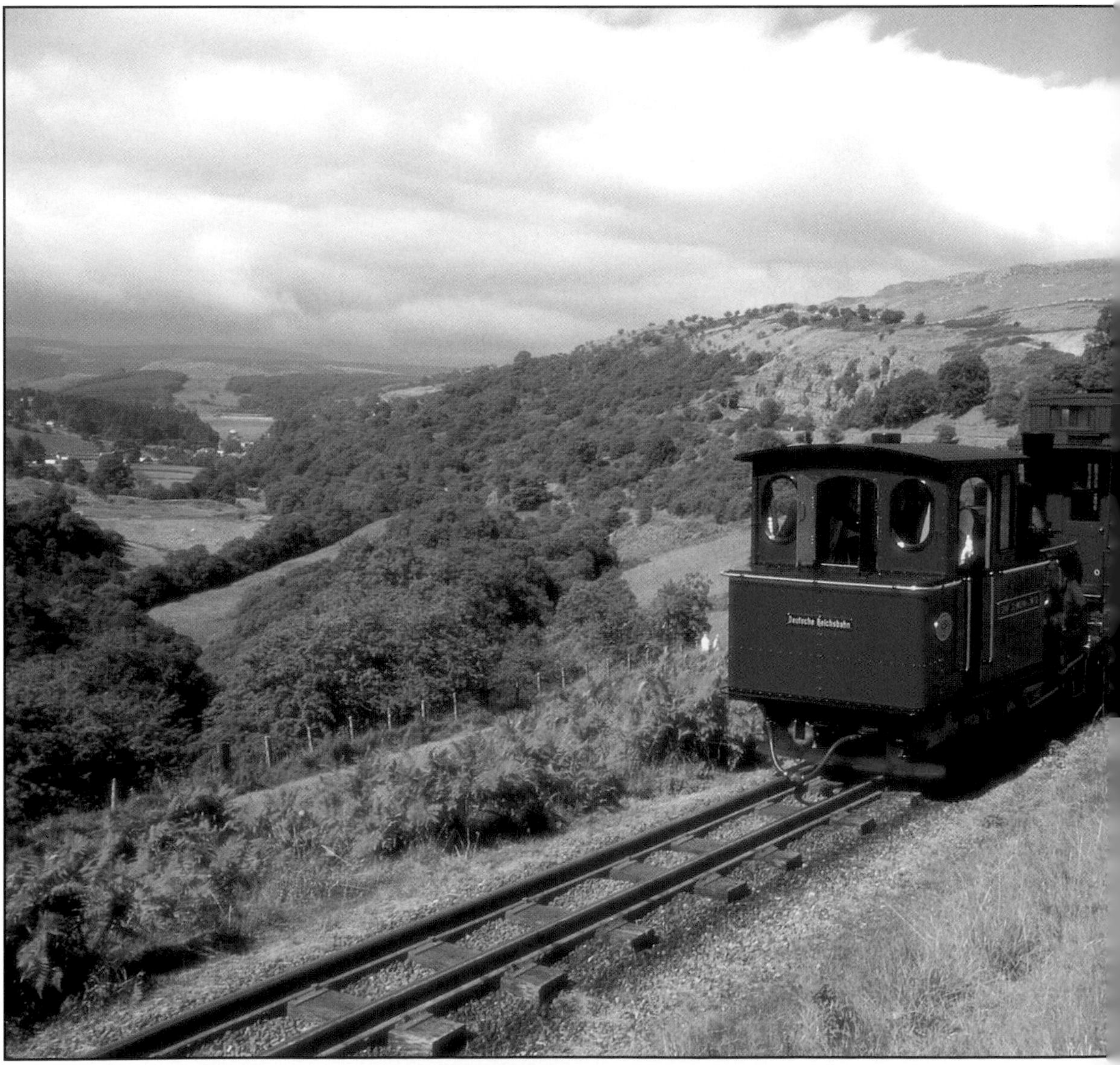

Passengers enjoy lovely views on the line. Pontsticill can be seen in the background

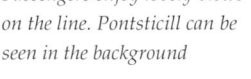

beautifully kept maroon *Graf Schwerin-Löwitz*, built in 1908 for a narrow gauge railway in eastern Germany. It usually hauls four observation coaches and a caboose based on a design for a narrow gauge railway in Maine, USA; this vehicle is ideal for visitors in wheelchairs. As the train pulls out, the remains of adjacent quarries to the west indicate the source of limestone for the ironworks which made Merthyr Tydfil famous.

The gleaming, much used Graf Schwerin-Löwitz

Evidence of quarrying can be seen at places throughout the 2-mile (3km) journey to the former junction at Pontsticill, but it does not detract from the grandeur of the scenery as the railway enters the Brecon Beacons National Park. Streams tumble down the wooded hillsides, some feeding the Taf Fechan reservoir, behind which three peaks of the Brecon Beacons rise up. The middle peak, Pen-y-Fan, is the highest in south Wales at 2907ft (886m). The reservoir holds 3400 million gallons and was built in 1927.

From Pontsticill there are attractive walks, including the trackbed of the line towards Dolygaer and the summit tunnel at Torpantau, along which the line will be extended in due course.

Train service: daily except Monday and Tuesday April-May; daily June to September; Sunday, Tuesday to Thursday October. Tel: 01685 722988.

The Cob at Porthmadog was built by a local landowner to relieve unemployment

FFESTINIOG RAILWAY
Gwynedd

PORTHMADOG, 18 MILES (29 KM) SOUTH OF CAERNARFON

*T*he history of the Ffestiniog Railway is reassuring evidence that events in the remotest of places can make a significant impact on world history. Testimony to this was given by no less a personage than the Russian Tsar, who sent the Ffestiniog's manager and engineer a gold medallion and silver shield in recognition of the railway's influence. The interest of Victorian railway engineers and builders in the Ffestiniog Railway was due to its narrow gauge of 1ft 1½in (600mm) and its pioneering use of steam locomotives.

But the railway would never have come into being at all had not William Madocks, local landowner and Member of Parliament for Boston in Lincolnshire, built the great embankment called the Cob across the estuary of Traeth Mawr, which was opened in 1811. This diverted water channels and led to the scouring of the natural harbour that became the slate transhipment dock of Port Madoc, now Porthmadog.

A 13½-mile (20km) railway was built to link Port Madoc with the slate quarries at Blaenau Ffestiniog, and the

Ffestiniog Railway opened in 1836 using gravity for the descent from Blaenau and horses to pull the empty wagons back up the hill. The horses recovered their strength while riding downhill in 'dandy' wagons. The growth in demand for slate, spurred by the Industrial Revolution and the growth of towns and cities, necessitated the adoption of steam for haulage. The Ffestiniog's manager, Charles Spooner, commissioned the London engineers George England & Co to design and build four small locomotives, the first for commercial use on such a small gauge. Two arrived in 1863 and the other two the following year. Passengers were first carried officially in 1865, their custom becoming ever more important to the railway as tourism flourished and slate carrying declined.

It was the next great innovation that was to attract the Tsar's emissary, Count Bobrinsky. In 1870 trials were held with a recently delivered double bogie steam locomotive designed by James Fairlie – its articulation permitted a long boiler with central firebox, and Fairlie's name was given to the type. Shortly afterwards the Ffestiniog Railway became not only the first narrow gauge railway to try bogie passenger coaches but one of the first railways in Britain to employ them. Descendants of this engine still take the Ffestiniog Railway's passengers from sea level up to 710ft (216m).

Passengers first rode on the railway in 1865

Harbour station, on the south-eastern edge of Porthmadog, contains a museum that helps passengers to derive far more from their journey than simply an appreciation of the glorious scenery. Crossing the Cob as the train leaves Porthmadog, a panorama of mountains including Snowdon can be seen to the north-east on a clear day. On the opposite side, waves lap the massive rocks that strengthen Madocks's work. As the line swings round through 90 degrees at the end of the Cob, the Ffestiniog's works and carriage and engine sheds can be seen to the right, named Boston Lodge after Madocks's constituency.

The climb begins here and barely lets up all the way to Blaenau. At the first station, Minffordd, the site of interchange sidings with the main line that runs along the coast can be seen to the left. Passengers can still conveniently change trains here. Beyond the single platform at Penrhyn the line enters the Snowdonia National Park. From here on the scenery is seldom less than spectacular, the line often twisting along the contours of the hills with long drops to the valley floor.

As the line approaches the isolated crossing station at Tan-y-Bwlch, a descending train can often be seen nearing the station on the opposite side of the valley. It was here during the 1930s and 1950s that the station mistress, Bessie Jones, attired in Welsh costume, dispensed home-made teas. A number of walks can be taken from Tan-y-Bwlch station, for which the operators thoughtfully provide a leaflet, *Where to go and what to do from Ffestiniog Railway stations*.

Dduallt station marks the beginning of the Deviation, forced on the railway by the submersion of the old trackbed by the lower reservoir of the pumped storage scheme near Tanygrisiau. Construction began in 1965 and people from all walks of life, many with no interest in railways, volunteered to help to build the new railway. It was no simple task, entailing construction of the only spiral on a public railway in Britain and a new Moelwyn Tunnel.

The old trackbed and tunnel mouth can be seen as the train climbs away from the loop and plunges into the 287yd (262m) tunnel. The train emerges to skirt Tanygrisiau Reservoir and squeeze past the backs of houses into Blaenau, the hills a jumble of slate and rock from two centuries of extraction. Journey's end is a new interchange

station opened with the help of British Rail and the county council, enabling passengers to reach the Ffestiniog Railway from the north Wales coast at Llandudno Junction.

Train service: daily from late March to early November; weekends in late February/March. Santa specials. Tel: 01766 512340.

Left: David Lloyd George, a double-bogie engine built in 1992 – one of the descendants of James Fairlie's innovations

Below: Tanygrisiau, the last stop before Blaenau

Want to be an Engine Driver?

There was a time when every boy wanted to be an engine driver when he grew up. For those who still harbour such atavistic ambitions, many preserved railways offer the chance to get your hands on the shovel and regulator. You can develop a sense of just what hard work it is to feed several tons of coal into a greedy firebox during a shift, or experience the thrill of the surge of power as the regulator is opened and steam rushes into the cylinders.

There are significant differences between the courses on offer around the country. The Nene Valley course is of two hours duration, the Keighley & Worth Valley four hours, the West Somerset two days. Some, like the Midland Railway Centre, the Battlefield Steam Railway and the Birmingham Railway Museum, offer a choice of two hours, half a day and a full day.

What they have in common is a preparatory talk about safety – the subject of paramount importance in all aspects of railway operations. This is usually followed by a talk about how steam locomotives work, the theory and practice of firing and the techniques of driving. On railways that have signal boxes, it is common

for those on longer courses to have a session with a signalman to learn how to interpret fixed and hand signals. Of course this condenses into hours what railwaymen took years to assimilate, so slow was progress through the grades from cleaner to top link driver.

Then comes the part that brings smiles to all – footplate experience. On longer courses, this will usually begin with pottering up and down outside the engine shed or in the goods yard. This is followed on railways (as opposed to centres) by a trip over the line; this can be a tall order for novices. Perhaps the most challenging is the 1 in 40 climb out of Bodmin Parkway on the Bodmin & Wenford Railway. Starting a matter of yards from the end of the platform, this can tax the skill of experienced drivers on a wet day.

Some railways broaden the course further, like that on the Gwili which takes in guard's duties and the full work of signalmen. However, for a weekend signalling course, it is

necessary to go to the Severn Valley Railway, where an educational charity, the Kidderminster Railway Museum, organises such courses. Participants receive initial instruction in the museum, followed by visits to the signal boxes on the railway. Contact the Kidderminster Railway Museum, Comberton Hill, Kidderminster, Worcestershire (tel: 01562 825316) for further information.

Being in control of a locomotive in full steam is the stuff of many a child's dream: in reality it is a skilled and arduous job. For those keen to give it a try, various taster courses are available around the country

GWILI RAILWAY
Dyfed

3 MILES (5 KM) NORTH OF CARMARTHEN

*A*t present the Gwili Railway is only 1¾ miles (3km) long, running from Bronwydd Arms to Llwyfan Cerrig, but what it lacks in length it makes up for in both scenery and the high standards it has set itself for the future. The plan is to extend the railway further north to Llanpumpsaint to give a run of about 8 miles (13km), and the Gwili Railway already owns the trackbed. As its name suggests, the line follows the River Gwili along a gently sloped valley, passing well-wooded hillsides and meadows on its way to Llwyfan Cerrig, where there is no road access but a picnic site to prolong your visit.

The basis of the railway is the long cross-country line once operated by the Great Western Railway between Aberystwyth and Carmarthen. This glorious line served such delightfully named places as Derry Ormond, Strata Florida and Caradog Falls Halt, taking three hours to cover the 60 miles (96.5km) due to the number of stations and the single track line. In the 1920s arriving passengers at Aberystwyth could even enjoy *thé dansant* on a sprung dance floor provided by the Great Western in its new station building. A flavour of the old days is reflected in the collection of period photographs in the waiting room.

The modern age had no place for such leisurely progress or pursuits. Passenger services ended in 1965 and the last freight was carried on the southern section in 1973, but the Gwili Railway stepped in to create what has become the first standard gauge preserved railway in Wales. Everything you see has been done by volunteers – tracklaying, dismantling and re-erecting railway buildings from elsewhere in Wales, as well as the restoration of carriages and locomotives. Help has been received from various sources – railway enthusiasts from Brynteg School, for example, have made a superb job of restoring an 1891 Taff Vale Railway coach that served for half a century as a farmer's shed in Herefordshire following its withdrawal

from service in 1926. Examine the flower-decorated signal box at Bronwydd Arms (the signalman welcomes visitors) which has been so well transposed from its original home at Llandybie on the Central Wales line that you would think it had always been here.

Train service: Sundays from May to September, also Wednesdays in June and daily from late July to August. Santa specials. Tel: 01267 231817.

Based at Bronwydd Arms station (left), trains follow part of the old GWR Carmarthen–Aberystwyth line; there are plans to extend the route

LLANBERIS LAKE RAILWAY
Gwynedd

LLANBERIS, 6 MILES (9.5 KM) EAST OF CAERNARFON

Built on the trackbed of the Padarn Railway which carried slate from the Dinorwic Quarries to the Menai Strait, the railway (opposite) follows the lake for much of its route.; Hunslet 0-4-0ST Dolbadarn (below) came from the quarries

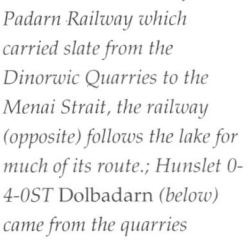

Slate was the original reason for the existence of most of today's tourist railways in north Wales, and a journey on the Llanberis Lake Railway can be combined with a visit to the adjacent Welsh Slate Museum, offering a marvellous insight into the industry's history. They are situated near the village of Llanberis, once home to many of the 3000 workmen employed at the nearby Dinorwic Quarries and also the start of the Snowdon Mountain Railway.

The Llanberis Lake Railway uses the trackbed of the former Padarn Railway, built to join the quarries to the harbour at Port Dinorwic, and the museum occupies the imposing slate building that formed the quarry and railway workshops. Besides a visit to the museum, it is worth allowing time to follow the trails around the spectacular Vivian Quarry, in which sheer walls of slate rise up from the flooded centre, and to look round the visitor centre in the former quarry hospital.

Trains are hauled by one of three 1ft 10¾in (576mm) gauge steam locomotives that once hauled slate wagons around the upper galleries at Dinorwic Quarries to the head of the inclined planes. The wagons were then lowered down to the larger 4ft (1200mm) Padarn Railway on which they were carried piggyback to waiting ships.

Llanberis Lake Railway trains leave from the station named Gilfach Ddu, beside the car park they share with the museum. The line soon enters a cutting through slate tips, leading to an impressive arch dated 1900. Beyond here the scenery opens out, and for the rest of the 40-minute round trip the line is seldom more than a few feet from the edge of Lake Padarn. The carriages allow almost unobstructed views across the water to the village of Llanberis and the slopes of Snowdon, on which a plume of steam can sometimes be seen as a Snowdon Mountain Railway train crawls up the mountain.

On the outward journey trains do not stop at the one intermediate station, Cei Llydan, nor is it possible to get out at the terminus at Penllyn while the locomotive uncouples and runs round the train. However, you can break the journey at Cei Llydan on the return, and there are picnic tables and benches beside the lake and in the trees on the opposite side of the line.

Train service: daily fom April to September, and on selected days in March and October. Tel: 01286 870549.

LLANGOLLEN RAILWAY
Denbighshire

LLANGOLLEN, 11 MILES (17.5 KM) NORTH OF OSWESTRY

M ost preserved railways have been saved partly because they pass through attractive countryside that visitors with no particular interest in railways would enjoy. It is certainly hard to beat the 5½-mile (8km) Llangollen Railway for the glorious landscapes that the railway offers its passengers during the 28-minute journey. Before closure by British Railways in 1964–8, the line was used by excursion trains of ramblers from towns in the north-west and by the 'North Wales Scenic Land Cruise' trains.

When work began on rebuilding the railway at the Eisteddfod town of Llangollen in 1975, the station had been derelict for over ten years and the track had been lifted. It must have seemed a daunting task to reach the target of Corwen, 10 miles (16km) away, but the Llangollen Railway is well over half way there and working on the next section, between the present terminus at Glyndyfrdwy and Carrog.

Standing on the sinuous platform at Llangollen, there is a sound of water trickling over rocks, which comes from the River Dee flowing beneath the southern platform. The 13th–14th-century bridge at the platform end provides a fine view of the station and the river with a backdrop of the Berwyn Hills through which the

Talking to interested passengers (below and opposite) is very much part of the job of anyone working with preserved railways

railway runs. Time should be allowed to explore the small town, overlooked by the remains of Castell Dinas Bran and famous for having been the home of the eccentric 'Ladies of Llangollen'. Their home at Plas Newydd, just to the south-west of the town, is open to the public.

As the train eases out of Llangollen, the former goods yard can be seen at a higher level on the right; once served by up to four daily goods trains, it is now the preserved line's engine shed and workshops, reached by a line from Llangollen Goods Junction, where a signal box and passing loop is now situated. Beyond here the line turns briefly away from the Llangollen Canal and crosses the Dee, which remains on the right for the rest of the journey.

Climbing steeply, the line passes Pentrefelin where sidings accommodated coaching stock from Eisteddfod and other excursions as well as acting as an interchange point for slate from Oernant quarry; they are now the base for diesel and coach restoration. In the days when the railways carried most of the nation's freight, whole trains of seeds were dispatched from these sidings after loading in the town's goods yard.

Railway, canal and river share a gorge on the approach to the ornate mock Tudor station at Berwyn, which was designed to complement the older part of the Chain Bridge Hotel, named after the suspension footbridge that sways over the Dee. It is only a

Pastoral scenery near Glyndyfrdwy, where there are good facilities for children

Leaving Berwyn station

ten-minute walk from the station, across the footbridge, to the Horseshoe Falls built by Thomas Telford. Their purpose was to supply water to the Shropshire Union Canal, of which the Llangollen Canal is a feeder. Walkers can obtain sustenance at Berwyn station's tea-room. Leaving the station, the train crosses a six-arch bridge followed by a view of the falls. Passengers are then treated to spectacular views of the river and Llantisilio Hall.

Leaving Berwyn Tunnel, at 689yds (630m) the third longest on a preserved railway, the line emerges on a ledge high above the river. On level ground is Deeside Halt where a passing loop was built as long ago as 1908 to split the section of single line between Llangollen Goods Junction and Glyndyfrdwy. Public footpaths

from the halt make it a good place to break the journey for a walk through riverside meadows.

The valley opens out as the railway approaches the present terminus at Glyndyfrdwy (pronounced Glin Duvver-Dwee), where a refreshment room, picnic area and children's playground are provided. Glyndyfrdwy was the birthplace of the 14th-century Welsh patriot Owain Glyndwr, who is regarded as one of the founders of Welsh nationalism. In recent years the station was known for its slate traffic from two local quarries, which was used for window sills, steps, lavatories and billiard tables and was brought to the railway by tramway.

Train service: daily from Whitsun to October, and weekends in February, March and April. Santa specials in December. Tel: 01978 860951.

Dining on the Rails

*T*here is something very special about the experience of having a meal served to you on board a train. Breakfasting aboard a London-bound train, for instance, as it skirts the sea between Teignmouth and Exeter, the sun just beginning to gild the waves, is a qualitative pleasure that no other form of transport can rival.

This attribute of railway travel has been put to good use by the preserved railways, with most of the larger railways now offering a range of possibilities for eating aboard specially equipped and appointed trains. The combination of pleasant and slowly changing scenery, steam locomotion and good food in an historic or comfortable coach (or both) has provided a valuable source of income for many lines. The fortunate railways were operating early enough to be able to buy Pullman coaches as they were sold off following the withdrawal of such services on British Rail. The Kent & East Sussex Railway has a particularly fine set of such vehicles; amongst the three cars of the Wealden Pullman is *Barbara*, built in 1926 and still with its original marquetry panelling.

One of the first railways to offer dining trains was the Great Central Railway, which has been able to draw on a nearby catering college for skilled volunteers. Other lines, like the Llangollen and the Ffestiniog railways, have set up a relationship with local caterers, restaurateurs or hotels. In conjunction with Hotel Maes-y-Neuadd, the Ffestiniog Railway offers a range of options, from lunch or dinner on the train to a hotel/special train package for large functions.

Each railway offers something slightly different, so it is advisable to contact the individual railway for

Right and opposite: the Berwyn Belle Luxury Pullman dining train, Llangollen Railway

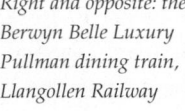

details. The Keighley & Worth Valley, for example, offers special dinners that take the 1920s or the 1940s and World War II as their theme. Visitors are encouraged to wear appropriate dress, and the six-course dinner is served by liveried stewards and stewardesses. The Mid-Hants Railway offers breakfast on certain days, and several railways offer afternoon tea. The Midland Railway Centre hosts children's parties and does the clearing up.

One of the two Brighton Belle Pullmans on the North Norfolk Railway runs to a piano to enliven pre-prandial drinks at the adjacent cocktail bar. The railway also prides itself on the provision of both gas and electricity in its large kitchen car, to ensure the chef can use the best form of heat for a particular dish, as well as the use of local fresh seafood. The Llangollen Railway and Midland Railway Centre have been quick to note the popularity of disco trains on some trans-European routes; the former offers a live band in a coach cleared for dancing, while the latter can add a disco coach on request.

Meals taken on board in style give journeys an extra dimension

GWR 2-8-0 No 2857, built in Swindon in 1918, at Kidderminster station

SEVERN VALLEY RAILWAY
Worcestershire/Shropshire

KIDDERMINSTER, 5½ MILES (9 KM) SOUTH OF STOURBRIDGE

The Severn Valley Railway has reason enough for its claim to be Britain's premier steam railway. At 16 miles (25km) in length, it is one of the longest lines; it passes through some of the most delightful scenery to be enjoyed on a tourist railway; the train service is busy enough at peak periods to require five trains in operation; its stations are superbly restored and quite individual in character; and it has one of the most varied collections of locomotives and rolling stock. Yet the character of a 1-hour 10-minute journey over the line can vary enormously. In common with other railways that operate a service for most of the year, the atmosphere fluctuates from that of a busy cross-country railway, with powerful tender engines pulling long trains during the high season, to a quiet country branch line off season.

Try a weekend in mid-March or even November, when the short trains are usually hauled by tank engines,

and stay until the last train of the day. At Highley, one of the smaller intermediate stations, only a handful of passengers await the train, the gas lamps cast an unfamiliar glow over the platform, and the only sounds are of birds in the wooded hillside above the station. The ring of bells in the signal box, the rustle of signal wires and the metallic drop of lever locks herald the arrival of your train. Its headlamps glowing, the engine rounds the curve with the orange glare from the firebox illuminating the driver and fireman. The cold air produces clouds of steam as the small-wheeled tank briskly climbs away to Bridgnorth. Such experiences are the essence of preserved railways.

For almost 20 years, from the arrival of the first locomotive and four carriages in 1967, the historic Shropshire town of Bridgnorth was the headquarters of the Severn Valley Railway. The line was progressively re-opened to the south until 1984 when the final section, from Bewdley to Kidderminster, reconnected the railway to the Railtrack network. By redeveloping the goods yard at the Worcestershire carpet town, the Severn Valley was able to build an imposing new terminus in traditional Great Western Railway style. Kidderminster then became the railway's main station, the minute's walk between the stations encouraging passengers to use the frequent trains from Birmingham. A connection with

As much care is given to the restoration and preservation of station buildings, signs and furniture as it is to the trains themselves

the Birmingham–Worcester line also enables through excursions on to the Severn Valley Railway. Before boarding a train, it is worth spending time in Kidderminster Railway Museum, which provides an introduction to all the paraphernalia that railway companies produced as part of their operations – from signal-box lever frames, which visitors can work, to the lunch boxes of footplate crews.

As departing trains negotiate the points at the station throat, they pass the new signal box on the left and the railway's turntable and storage sidings on the right. The exit from Kidderminster is unremarkable, passing a sugar beet factory that was the line's last source of freight traffic, but once through a 480yd (439m) tunnel, the line enters a wholly different landscape. Heathland borders the line until the approach to Bewdley, where the animals of West Midlands Safari Park can usually be seen. The home town of the former prime minister Stanley Baldwin is well worth an hour or two's exploration on foot: it has some fine vernacular buildings of medieval and Georgian origin and a remarkably good museum illustrating such local crafts as rope-making and honey farming. The station here was once the junction for lines to Hartlebury and to Tenbury Wells, accounting for its three platforms. Good views of the town and Telford's bridge of 1801 can be had from the eight-arch viaduct to the north of the station.

Colourful sails try to catch the breeze on Trimpley Reservoir, skirted by the railway before it descends through woods to the engineering highlight of the line – the Victoria Bridge. Designed by John Fowler (who later designed the Forth Bridge) and cast by the famous Coalbrookdale Company, the 200ft (60m) span was the longest cast-iron clear span in the world when it was completed in 1861. It is worth disembarking at the next station, Arley, for a pleasant walk beside the River Severn, which is seldom out of view for the rest of the journey, back to the bridge to admire

its construction and its idyllic setting.

The valley of the Severn is remarkably unspoilt as the train presses north through Highley station to Hampton Loade, to which generations of anglers have travelled from Birmingham over the years, and where a river ferry gives access to the opposite bank and its riverside pubs. Beyond the closed halt at Eardington, a bend in the river increases its distance from the line as it traverses a deep cutting and short tunnel. A succession of bridges and viaducts precedes journey's end at Bridgnorth, where the old town can be reached by the footbridge from the station.

Train service: daily during Easter week, and from May to September; October half term, weekends in March, October and November. Santa specials. Tel: 01299 403816/0800 600 900.

*Refuelling with water (as
seen left) is a regular job,
especially when a good head
of steam has been raised
Below: pulling out of Arley*

SNOWDON MOUNTAIN RAILWAY

Gwynedd

LLANBERIS, 6 MILES (9.5 KM) EAST OF CAERNARFON

*I*n comparison with the Alps, Britain's peaks are pretty lowly affairs, but the grandeur of Snowdon, the highest mountain in England and Wales, has long attracted the fittest walkers. Until 1896 they were the only people to scale its slopes, but on 6 April 1896 the 2ft 7½in (800mm) gauge Snowdon Mountain Railway began operations from Llanberis to the Summit station. It was a sad day for the promoters, for a locomotive derailed and plummeted down the mountainside. Fitting an additional safety device delayed opening for another year, but since then the railway has operated without incident and carried millions of passengers up the 3560ft (1085m) mountain.

The Snowdon Mountain Railway is Britain's only rack railway – that is, one equipped with a double-bladed toothed bar between the rails; this is engaged by a cog on the locomotive which claws its way up the mountain. It is worth examining both the point-work and the mechanism on the steam locomotives to appreciate the skill of the Swiss engineers who built them, based on a system first used in the United States almost 130 years ago and perfected on numerous railways in Switzerland.

The station at Llanberis is close to

For many, the Snowdon railway is the classic 'Great Little Train of Wales'

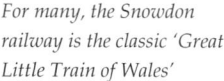

the ruins of the 13th-century Dolbadarn Castle at the east end of the village. It is advisable to take warm clothing on the 2½-hour round trip, for the weather can change quickly and in severe circumstances the train may not proceed to the summit. But on clear days you can see as far as the Isle of Man and the Wicklow Mountains of Ireland, and the views of the surrounding mountains are breathtaking. For much of the upper section, the railway is built on a ridge, affording a panorama on both sides. Even before the first public train of the day, a special train with staff and supplies for the summit cafeteria, as well as any shepherds and their dogs needing to round up sheep on the slopes, will have struggled up the mountain.

Four new acquisitions from Hunslet in Leeds have ended the monopoly of steam on the railway. The diesels enable the railway to provide a more flexible service, responding to a sudden improvement in the weather by laying on more trains. On busy days, it is as well to remember that you are guaranteed a seat only on the train by which you ascended, allowing no more than half an hour or so on the summit.

Train service: daily from mid-March to the end of October. Tel: 01286 870223.

Llanberis station, with one of the more recent diesel trains

TALYLLYN RAILWAY
Gwynedd

TYWYN, 15 MILES (24 KM) WEST OF MACHYNLLETH

Opposite: 0-4-2ST No1, Talyllyn, built in 1865, topping up with water at Tywyn before the climb up to Nant Gwernol

It would be hard to overestimate the importance of the Talyllyn Railway in the history of preserved railways throughout the world, for it was the very first such line. The inaugural meeting to save the moribund railway was held in Birmingham in 1950, and a service was run by volunteers from the following year. Its successful formula has been emulated in other countries, from the United States to New Zealand.

But the Talyllyn's distinguished place in the annals of tourist railways might be of little account to today's visitors were it not one of the most characterful of narrow gauge railways. The unusual 2ft 3in (686mm) gauge line threads its way up the south side of the valley of the River Fathew, most of it within the Snowdonia National Park. For much of its length it runs along a shelf in the hillside, affording views across the valley and towards the dominant peak of Cader Idris. But there are also wooded sections around Dolgoch (alight for a walk to the falls) and on the final part beyond Abergynolwyn to the terminus at Nant Gwernol.

It was to link the slate quarries at Bryn Eglwys above Nant Gwernol with the main line railway at Tywyn that the railway was opened in 1866. At the terminus a new footbridge across the precipitous ravine and woodland trails enable visitors to explore the remains of the quarries and abandoned village, which were joined to the railway by rope-worked inclined planes.

Besides the charm of its simple stations and the scenery, the Talyllyn Railway is fortunate in having seven very different steam locomotives, including the two original to the line, albeit frequently rebuilt. If they seem familiar, it may be because several have been the basis of characters in the Reverend W Awdry's books for children: *Sir Haydn* appears as 'Sir Handel', *Edward Thomas* as 'Peter Sam', *Talyllyn* as 'Skarloey' and *Douglas* as 'Duncan' in stories about the Skarloey (Talyllyn) Railway.

It would take an expert to distinguish between the line's original coaches, which are used on Heritage trains during September weekends, and the more recent products of the Talyllyn's carriage works at Pendre. The overall appearance is very similar, but the older vehicles are usually four-wheelers. An exception is the observation car, No 17, which was used on the nearby Corris Railway until 1930, when it was sold for use as a garden shed and greenhouse. Now restored to its original brown livery, it provides the clearest views from the railway during the 55-minute journey.

Train service: daily from late March to October, and Sundays from mid-February to late March. Santa specials. Tel: 01654 710472.

VALE OF RHEIDOL RAILWAY
Ceredigion

ABERYSTWYTH, 17 MILES (27 KM) SOUTH OF MACHYNLLETH

*T*he 1ft 11½in (597mm) Vale of Rheidol Railway from Aberystwyth to Devil's Bridge had the distinction of being the last steam-worked line on British Rail, surviving the demise of standard gauge steam in 1968. Since nationalisation in 1948, interest in making a success of the line had waxed and waned, but in 1988 a decision was taken to sell the railway. Bought by the owners of the Brecon Mountain Railway, it has been operated by them since April 1989.

Amongst the Welsh narrow gauge lines, the Vale of Rheidol was unusual in developing its tourist potential right from its opening in 1902, as well as fulfilling the primary purpose of transporting lead ore to the coast. It was built to a narrow gauge because standard gauge would have been prohibitively costly to build – as the one-hour journey quickly makes evident.

Most passengers join the train at Aberystwyth, where the Vale of

GWR 2-6-2T No 9, Prince of Wales, passes along the Rheidol valley, near Capel Seion

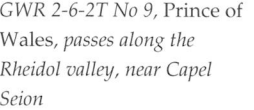

Rheidol leaves from a bay platform in the main line station. The days when the Great Western Railway held *thé dansants* on a sprung dance floor at Aberystwyth station are long gone, and it is now the main line that is the poor relation of the preserved railway. Its smartly turned-out trains have at least three times the number of carriages as those bound for Shrewsbury.

For much of the 11¾ mile (19km) journey the line clings to the hillside on a sinuous ledge with awesome drops below. Woods sheath the upper part of the line, so spring or mid-autumn are the better seasons for views across the valley, once spanned by an aerial cableway that brought lead to the station at Rhiwfron. Unless a request stop is made at one of the seven intermediate stations, the only pauses in the slog up the hill are normally at Nantyronen for the sturdy tank locomotive to take water, and in high season at Aberffrwd to pass a descending train.

Time should be allowed to admire the three bridges, one above the other at the summit. They span a whirlpool known as the Devil's Punchbowl. The oldest, at the lowest level, was completed by monks in 1087. About 1½ hours should be allowed for a visit to the Mynach waterfalls, which includes steep climbs.

Train service: April and October daily, except Monday and Friday; May Saturday to Thursday; daily June to August. Tel: 01970 625819.

Devil's Bridge, reached after a steep 4-mile (6.4km) climb

WELSHPOOL & LLANFAIR RAILWAY
Powys

WELSHPOOL, 16 MILES (25.5 KM) WEST OF SHREWSBURY

*T*he Welshpool & Llanfair Railway is a survivor of an oddity in Britain – the general purpose narrow gauge railway. The few lines that were built to narrow gauge, mostly in Wales, had a specific traffic to justify their construction, but from its opening in 1903 until closure in 1956, this 2ft 6in (762mm) gauge line carried general merchandise and the district's products, such as livestock, timber and flour. It even carried passengers until bus competition brought that service to an end in 1931.

Unfortunately the section through the large market town of Welshpool, linking with the main line station on the Shrewsbury–Aberystwyth line, ran between the houses and was not available. So the terminus of the 8-mile (12km) line at Llanfair Caereinion became the headquarters.

Joan, *built in 1927 in Stoke-on-Trent, spent most of its life hauling sugar cane in Antigua before being bought for the W&L in 1971*

The locomotives maintained there are an intriguing mix. Besides the two tank engines built for the line, *The Earl* and *The Countess*, there are locomotives rescued from railways in Austria, Finland, West Africa and Antigua as well as other British lines. With some of them came coaches, and a highlight of a 45-minute journey is to stand on the balcony of one of the Austrian coaches as the locomotive tackles the fierce 1 in 29 gradient out of Welshpool.

The scenery is a joy, for the sparsely inhabited pastoral landscape has lost none of its charm under the onslaught of modern agriculture. Woods still cover much of the broad, shallow valley, including the peripheral woodland of the Powis Castle estate, and towards Llanfair you can see the mills that once ground flour beside the River Banwy. The bridge carrying the line over the river nearly spelt disaster to the fledgling preservationists. The winter after re-opening of the line in 1963, storms seriously damaged the bridge, but thanks to help from army engineers and the public response to an appeal fund, the bridge was rebuilt the following summer.

At Llanfair visitors have the opportunity to look at the Welshpool & Llanfair's locomotives and rolling stock, and wonder at the extraordinary contrast between the massive 2-6-2T from the Jokioisten Railway in Finland and the diminutive No 8 *Dougall* which worked at a gasworks in Glasgow. It is hard to believe they run on the same gauge.

Train service: selected days from mid-April to October; daily for seven weeks from mid-July. Santa specials. Tel: 01938 810441.

A landscape hardly changed in centuries accompanies the line

The National Railway Museum, York

✳

*P*reserved railways are wonderful at re-creating the atmosphere of the steam railway and at giving those who have never seen a steam engine at work an idea of their appeal. But what they cannot do is to place railways in an economic and social context. For a lively introduction to the way railways have developed from rudimentary beginnings and changed the world, the National Railway Museum cannot be bettered.

Only ten minutes' walk from York station, the museum is now the largest railway museum in the world. It opened in 1975 following the amalgamation of the earlier small museum at York with the large collection from Clapham in London. A major expansion opened in 1992, allowing exhibits to be placed in a more authentic setting in the South Building, once the North Eastern Railway goods shed. Entitled

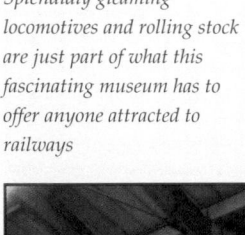

Splendidly gleaming locomotives and rolling stock are just part of what this fascinating museum has to offer anyone attracted to railways

'Travelling by Train', the display illustrates the way the experience and quality of train travel has evolved by matching locomotives and carriages of the same period and surrounding them with contemporary artefacts.

This has allowed the displays in the original Great Hall to concentrate on the technology of railways, presenting themes which try to foster an understanding of the various components of the railway. Sections on track and signalling show how the quest for safety has driven innovation and made railways by far the safest form of land transport. A reconstruction of Wolverton works manager's office is part of an introduction to the absorbing subject of railway workers, from navvy to general manager.

The impact of railways on the carriage of mail, on royal travelling habits, holidays, civil engineering,

steamer services – all are presented in imaginative displays that convey their information in a light and interesting way. But the greatest space is devoted to locomotives and rolling stock, of which the museum has an unparalleled collection, ranging from a working replica of *Rocket* to the prototype High Speed Train power car, from the horse-drawn carriage of 1863 that worked at Port Carlisle to the royal saloon built in 1941 for HM Queen Elizabeth, now the Queen Mother. A star attraction is inevitably the world's fastest steam locomotive, *Mallard*, which topped 126mph (201kph), and there is a cutaway locomotive which shows the inner workings of a steam engine.

Exhibits are sometimes loaned out and others borrowed from preserved railways, and special exhibitions are put on each year, so regular visitors will always see something new. In school holidays there are sometimes theatrical events in which moments in railway history are re-enacted. The range of exhibits and the stories behind them are so varied that it would be astonishing if there was not plenty to appeal to everyone.

Museum open daily except 24–26 December. Tel: 01904 621261.

❊

EAST LANCASHIRE RAILWAY

Greater Manchester/Lancashire

BURY, 6 MILES (9.5 KM) WEST OF ROCHDALE

❊

*T*his 8½ -mile (13.5km) line is an eye-opener to anyone who thinks of the industrial part of Lancashire as being irredeemably spoilt by the past. Following the course of the River Irwell for its whole length, the line passes through the attractive Rossendale Valley with well-wooded hills and a network of footpaths for those who wish to explore the valley. Yet there is hardly a mile of the East Lancashire Railway where

sidings did not feed into the line from adjacent mills or quarries. Today, though, you will need someone who knows the area's history, or a good guide book and a sharp eye, to identify their remains, which diminish with each summer's growth. Some cotton mills still stand, but few serve their original purpose and most are converted to flats or are used by small businesses. The days when the railway tapped these countless sources of

No 5407 (below and opposite) on the relatively newly opened (1987) East Lancashire line

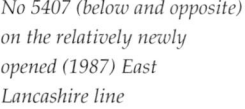

traffic and took their products for export all over the world seem almost as remote as the packhorse trains and canal barges which preceded them.

The most interesting and relaxing way to reach the southern terminus of the line at Bury Bolton Street station is by Metrolink, the light rail network that runs from Altrincham through the centre of Manchester to Bury. The short walk between the two stations can pass the Art Gallery & Museum, which has a remarkable collection of Victorian paintings, including work by Turner. The station at Bolton Street is typical of the secondary town station, with two platforms and loops for through trains. East Lancashire trains may well be hauled by visiting locomotives – as a comparatively recent addition to the ranks of tourist railways, most of its own locomotives from Barry are still under restoration.

Departing trains almost immediately enter a short tunnel, its northern portal crenellated to commemorate the medieval castle that was excavated when the tunnel was built.

The railway passes close to Peel Mill, once owned by the Peel family whose best-known member, Robert, became Prime Minister and founder of the police force (hence 'peelers'). The first station is at Summerseat, an industrial village dominated by the East Lancashire Railway's 13-span, 200yd (182m) Brooksbottom Viaduct. The listed Hoyle Mill is now converted into luxury flats, and the adjacent mill offices and pump room, which straddle the River Irwell, have been converted into a pub and restaurant.

The second tunnel after Summerseat has an unusual north portal: Nuttall Tunnel was built at the insistence of the owner of Nuttall Hall so that the railway would not impede his view of the river; the East Lancashire's directors decided to make a virtue out of necessity and create an elaborate turretted and crenellated face to the tunnel, into which were set what are thought to be carved faces of the directors. The expanse of Nuttall Park can be seen to the east as you cross a 275yd (251m) girder viaduct. The Grant family that lived at Nuttall Hall was immortalised by Charles Dickens as the Cheeryble Brothers in *Nicholas Nickleby*. The park, which is now publicly owned, can be easily visited

Ramsbottom station, faithfully and attractively rebuilt

on foot from the next station at Ramsbottom. This picturesque town is well worth exploring with the help of a leaflet for a walk that takes in the Ramsbottom Heritage Centre and other sites of interest. There are also walks up Holcombe Hill to the commemorative Peel Tower, with various pubs en route for refreshment.

Leaving Ramsbottom the train passes the site of extensive sidings and runs along an embankment with the river on the right. The valley narrows before the former junction at Stubbins where the main line to Accrington continued straight ahead, while the East Lancashire swings to the right. It appears that the line is dropping down, but this illusion is caused simply by the steeper gradient of the Accrington line to the west – in fact the East Lancashire line climbs steadily all the way from Bury to journey's end at Rawtenstall. Look out for the imposing Alberbottom Viaduct on the

Accrington line: its poor structural condition ended proposals to re-open this route.

Irwell Vale station is another good starting point for walks (booklets are available at Bury and Rawtenstall Tourist Information Centres). As well as the Irwell Valley Way, there are easy routes from here to Helmshore Textile Museum and Mill and to Stubbins Nature Reserve. The Irwell Way Sculpture Trail has works by British and foreign artists punctuating a pleasant walk.

The historic town of Rawtenstall, with its mill shops, market hall, Whitaker Park and the Rossendale Museum, also has Britain's last temperance bar, where you can sample such ancient recipes as black beer or dandelion and burdock.

Train service: weekends and bank holidays; also Fridays from mid-July to August. Santa specials. Tel: 0161-764 7790.

Nearly 750,000 passengers have travelled on the railway since it re-opened: the Bury to Ramsbottom section in 1987, Ramsbottom to Rawtenstall in 1991

ISLE OF MAN
STEAM RAILWAY
Isle of Man

DOUGLAS

*F*or a small island of 220 square miles (570 sq km), the Isle of Man is well blessed with surviving railways, and no visitor to the island should leave without a journey on at least one. The Manx Electric Railway continues in its second century of operation to perform an important transport function, linking the capital of Douglas with Ramsey; the Snaefell Mountain Railway, Britain's only electric mountain railway, takes visitors to the 2036ft (620m) summit; and the island's newest railway, the Groudle Glen, is a reconstruction of the Victorian railway that took visitors to a sea lion pool and bear pit, using one of the original locomotives

But those in search of steam head for the 3ft (900mm) gauge Isle of Man Steam Railway, which runs from Douglas to the seaside resort of Port Erin. The 15⅝-mile (24.5km) line is the last route of the Isle of Man Railway that once also served Peel, Foxdale and Ramsey. Even this remnant nearly closed during the late 1960s and early '70s, but the more farsighted members

of Tynwald, the island's parliament, urged its retention and in 1976 the government agreed to buy it.

The railway is now an intrinsic part of the island's tourist industry, and the Year of the Railway celebrations in 1993 brought tens of thousands to the island to ride on the various lines and the special trains. The reason for that enthusiasm is easy to understand after taking the train from Douglas to Port Erin. You will be hauled by one of the original little tank engines – once there were 15, the first arriving on the island for the opening of the first line, to Peel, in 1873. The carriages are also original Isle of Man stock, though many have been rebuilt or at least reupholstered.

The station is still imposing, built like others on the Port Erin line in the distinctive Ruabon brick, but it is no longer easy to see how the station once handled 100 trains a day, since the platforms have been reduced in number. The 65-minute journey is as delightful as ever, the steep gradients of the Port Erin line reflecting the rolling hills and eliciting a vigorous exhaust beat from the locomotive. Before the first station

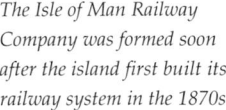
The Isle of Man Railway Company was formed soon after the island first built its railway system in the 1870s

is reached at Port Soderick, passengers enjoy views over the coast and can still disembark there to visit the beach and cove. Passing through woods, where in early summer there are fine displays of rhododendrons, you reach Castletown with its magnificent medieval fortress of Castle Rushen, before the unspoilt town of Port Erin. The station here offers not only a museum about the railway, but also good cakes in the station tea-room.

Train service: daily from April to October. Santa specials. Tel: 01624 662525.

The original tank engines still operate on the hour-long trip

Tramways

The return of electric trams, or light rail vehicles as their modern successors are termed, to the streets of Britain has rekindled interest in the history of the cleanest form of powered urban transport yet invented. Newspaper pictures of modern light rail vehicles in Manchester and Sheffield prompted many an editor to indulge in a local retrospective about the trams that once served their area.

Fortunately there are specialist museums or tramways where they can be seen at work, though with one exception they are not as well known as preserved steam railways. That exception is the National Tramway Museum at Crich in Derbyshire, which is the leading museum of its kind, probably in the world. Not only has it rescued over 40 trams from as far afield as Johannesburg, New York and Prague, but it has dismantled civic and urban buildings of all sizes and types and re-erected them to create an authentic setting for the trams. They operate over 2 miles (3km) of track that leaves the 'town' and winds its way round the hills overlooking Cromford.

They even have a steam tram which was built in 1885 and worked in Sydney, Australia. Wherever tram systems opened with steam, they were almost invariably converted to electricity, the only exceptions being in such exotic places as Surabaya in Java where steam trams survived until 1978. None of the older urban transport networks still exist, but several lines built primarily for tourists have survived. The most famous is the seafront tramway at Blackpool, which has become as much of an attraction as the tower, and runs for 12 miles (19km) along the front and on to Fleetwood.

The two separately worked lines on the Isle of Man, the Manx Electric and the Snaefell Mountain Railway, were both built for their tourist potential, but the former also provides useful transport between Douglas and Ramsey. It connects at Derby Castle with the Douglas Horse Tramway, which operates along the sea front. All three offer marvellous views and tramcars that are often original. In the case of the Snaefell Mountain, all but

The Isle of Man's electric tramway, which operates between Douglas and Ramsey

one of its six cars have been taking tourists up its 1 in 12 gradients to the summit since 1895. To climb such gradients in safety, they are fitted with a Fell centre-rail – a toothed rail between the running lines engaged by a cog on the tramcar.

An oddity is the 2ft 9in (838mm) gauge Seaton & District Electric Tramway, since its tramcars are built using mechanical and electrical parts salvaged from scrapped tramcars. The journey takes you inland from the Devon resort along the valley of the River Axe.

Trams and tower – where else but Blackpool!

A variety of locomotives ply this thriving branch line., including London Midland & Scottish 0-6-0T No 47279

KEIGHLEY & WORTH VALLEY RAILWAY
West Yorkshire

KEIGHLEY, 9 MILES (14.5 KM) WEST OF BRADFORD

After a journey on the Keighley & Worth Valley Railway, it's hard to believe that the line is only 4¾ miles (7.5km) long – it feels twice that length. It may be the three-and-a-half intermediate stations or the twistingvalley that delude one's senses, but the railway offers visitors much more than its length would suggest. This is one of the oldest standard gauge preserved railways, having opened to passengers six weeks before the end of steam on British railways in 1968, and six years after the line was closed down. The society that still runs the railway – one of the most democratic of any preserved railway – had come into being when the late Bob Cryer, MP, called a public meeting soon after closure to passengers.

What really put the line on the map was its use for the filming of *The Railway Children* in 1969. Based on the novel by E Nesbit, and starring Jenny Agutter and Bernard Cribbins, the film brought tens of thousands of visitors to the railway. Its unique atmosphere and its wide range of stock has ensured the frequent use of the railway by film and television companies, notably the use

of Keighley for the emotional departure scene in *Yanks* with Richard Gere.

One of the advantages of being in the vanguard of railway preservation was that the Keighley & Worth Valley and its supporting societies were able to acquire some very choice examples of both locomotives and rolling stock. Amongst them are carriages built as long ago as the 1870s, such as the Lancashire & Yorkshire Railway Directors' Saloon and the beautifully restored Great Central Railway four-wheeled coach in which HRH The Duchess of York has travelled. Such gems are used only on special occasions, but even the most modern carriage on the railway dates from 1961.

Parking at stations in the valley is very limited, so it is best to begin a journey at Keighley, which can be reached by frequent West Yorkshire Metro trains from Leeds and Bradford. Other than a renewal of signs, little seems to have changed on platform four since the Midland Railway rebuilt the whole of Keighley station in 1883. The period W H Smith outlet shelters under the ornately bracketed canopy that follows the gentle curve of the platform as it points up the valley. This curve, compounded by the 1 in 66 gradient, proved the undoing of the opening train in 1867, which slipped ignominiously to a standstill. The resourceful driver, however, reversed

Oxenhope ticket office recalls times gone by

right through the station to take a good run at it and conquered the slope without further embarrassment. The climb to Ingrow is still a test for engine crews, and the line continues to climb all the way to Oxenhope. Some of the mills that provided much of the line's goods traffic can still be seen here and there up the valley, but many have gone.

Ingrow station has been transformed since the early 1980s when it had a derelict air, the original vandalised station having been demolished. Thanks principally to the generosity of a society member, a Midland Railway stone station building in Lancashire was dismantled and re-erected here, oil lamps were installed and the stout entrance gates were recovered from a Keighley goods yard when it was replaced by a supermarket.

Pausing briefly at the request stop of Damems, reputedly the smallest railway station in Britain, the train soon enters Damems passing loop, specially put in by the Keighley & Worth Valley Railway to increase the number of trains that can be operated. Pasture edged with stone walls and well dotted with trees lines the railway as it climbs to Oakworth station, where Mr Perks held court in *The Railway Children*. The gas lamps, enamelled advertising signs, milk churns and the superbly restored interior make the station a period delight. The train soon reaches one of the favourite places for photographers, the three-arch Mytholmes Viaduct seen from the top of the tunnel of the same name and the scene of several sequences in that memorable film. After passing the huge mass of Ebor Mill, Haworth is reached, where many leave the train either to visit the locomotive shed and workshops or to explore the home town of the Brontë sisters. The enduring fascination of the literary family has made the mill town the focus of a major tourist industry.

There is a lovely walk between Haworth and the terminus at Oxenhope that follows the railway, crossing a 17th-century packhorse bridge and affording sight of 'Three Chimneys', used as the home of the Railway Children. Walkers can enjoy refreshments at Oxenhope and look round the museum, where some of the line's most historic vehicles and locomotives are kept, before taking the train home from the delightful station.

Train service: daily from June to the end of August, and weekends throughout the year. Tel: 01535 647777/645214.

Below: Oxenhope, one of the line's six immaculately kept stations

Opposite: the sheds at Haworth, a mill town made famous by the Brontës

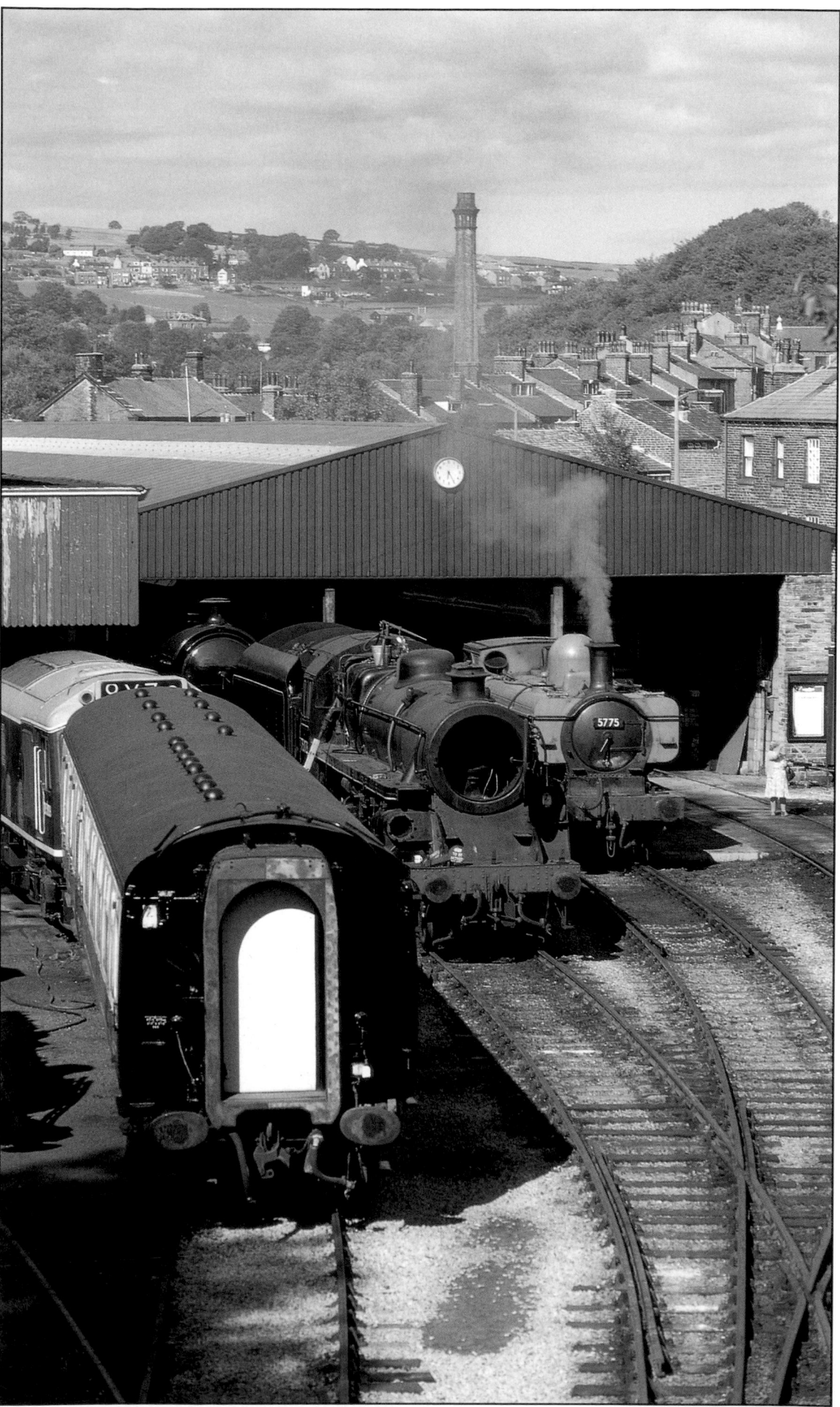

LAKESIDE & HAVERTHWAITE RAILWAY
Cumbria

STAVELEY, 9 MILES (14.5 KM) SOUTH OF WINDERMERE

*I*t is a cruel irony that the Lake Poets, and in particular Wordsworth, created a fascination for the romantic beauty of the district and then felt compelled to turn their pens to resisting the means whereby large numbers could enjoy it. However, it was the other railway to reach the shore of Windermere, the still open Kendal & Windermere, that was the subject of Wordsworth's vitriolic poem. By the time the Furness Railway

reached Lakeside in 1869, Wordsworth had been dead for 19 years.

The headquarters of the 3½-mile (5.5km) Lakeside & Haverthwaite Railway is at the latter station, curiously positioned between two unlined tunnels, like the bizarrely sited stations beside the Ligurian Sea between Genoa and La Spezia. The original idea was to connect with the main railway line further south at Plympton, but a road-widening scheme

Repulse approaching Newby Bridge halt

put paid to it. The tank locomotives that operate the line have a stiff climb out of Haverthwaite, running parallel with a line that served Backbarrow Ironworks until it closed in 1967. The finest views are over the Leven Valley to the east of the line, with the river frequently in sight. A large factory producing ultramarine (Reckitt's Blue) is passed on the right, and – more picturesquely – a waterfall and adjacent mill can be seen before the small halt at Newby Bridge is reached. It was while staying at the Newby Bridge Hotel in 1931 that Arthur Ransome wrote *Swallows and Amazons*. The halt, used during World War II to bring prisoners to the Grizedale Hall prisoner-of-war camp, is the start of a number of fine walks. But visitors should not miss the section of the line from here to Lakeside for it is the most scenic part, passing through oakwoods and skirting the

southern end of Lake Windermere.

The station buildings provided by the Furness Railway for its train and steamer services at Lakeside were so splendid that some shareholders complained of extravagance. Sadly they were almost entirely demolished before the Lakeside & Haverthwaite took over. However, steamers still connect with trains for a 3¼-hour cruise of the lake, which can be prolonged by visiting the Windermere Steam Boat Museum. Amongst the elegant vessels in its collection is the steam yacht *Esperance*, which Arthur Ransome immortalised as the houseboat in *Swallows and Amazons*.

Train service: Easter week and April weekends, then daily from late April to October. Tel: 015395 31594.

Waiting at Haverthwaite station

Pickering Castle, a well-preserved motte-and-bailey construction

A WALK AT PICKERING

❧

*P*ickering's romantic 12th-century castle provides the focal point for this walk on the edge of the North York Moors National Park; but additional attractions which can be combined with the walk include a steam-hauled trip on the North Yorkshire Moors Railway or a visit to the Beck Isle Folk Museum.

The walk is 2 miles (3km) long, through woods with oak, ash, rowan and whitebeam, and wood anemones and yellow pimpernel on the ground below. The walking is relatively easy, but there are some stony woodland paths, with uphill sections, and several stiles to cross. There is an informal picnic area by the castle walls, and a really delightful streamside picnic area in front of the Beck Isle Museum.

The walk starts at the crossroads and bridge below Pickering station. There are plenty of well-signed car parks in Pickering and at the castle, but all can be busy on summer weekends.

🐌🐌🐌🐌

DIRECTIONS

Cross the bridge to the Beck Isle Museum and picnic area, then go through a gate along the track to the left of the museum (marked 'Riding Stables'). Go through a gate to the left and along the broad, grassy track past the stables. Soon the path veers right to continue beside the beck and over a stile – ignore a concrete footbridge on the right.

Turn left, away from the beck, over rough pasture towards a wood ahead. Enter the wood by another stile, crossing a track into a caravan site, before following a narrow path between trees

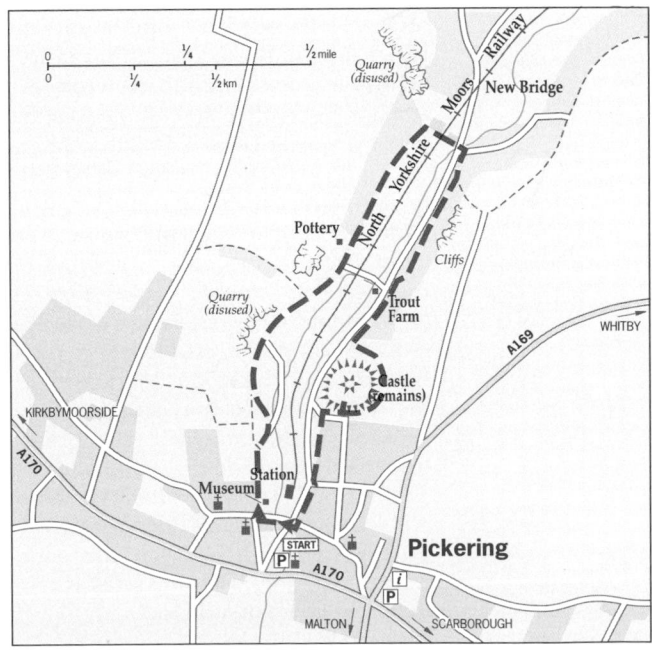

to exit at a stile. Bear half-right across a ridged field, and at the top go through the right-hand of two field gates on to a stony track.

Follow the track by woods, crossing a stile beside a gate (waymarked) and a farmhouse (now a pottery). The way narrows between hedges to a metal gate, then a second gate, before curving right across a field towards cottages.

Turn right through the gate by these cottages (waymarked) and right again to a path leading to a pedestrian gate across the railway line (look out for trains) and a footbridge over the stream. Follow the path to the road.

Cross the road and bear right to a path into the woods, which climbs the embankment parallel to the road. It soon joins a broader path from the left, passing limestone cliffs on the left. At a fork keep left, joining another track parallel to the road, and avoiding a path bearing right to the road. Keep to this path, with more cliffs on your right, to reach another fork. Bear right here to join the road with care, and cross to the other side. Pass a trout farm on the beck. Turn left for 250m (822ft) to a wooden barrier and footpath sign, taking a path on the opposite side of the road. Follow an old wall

away from the road up an incline by the edge of the wood. Where the wall ends go left for 10m (32ft), then right to where paths split below the castle walls. Head right then left up to the castle walls, circling left to the main entrance, then bearing right down-steps. Turn left down Castle Road to return to Pickering centre.

Pickering station is the start point of the popular North Yorkshire Moors Railway

NORTH YORKSHIRE MOORS RAILWAY
North Yorkshire

PICKERING, 16½ MILES (26.5 KM) WEST OF SCARBOROUGH

Goathland (opposite, top) and Grosmont (opposite, bottom) – two of just five stations on this long line

The appreciation of landscapes may be subjective, but few would argue with the claim that the scenery enjoyed by visitors to the North Yorkshire Moors Railway is some of the finest on any preserved railway. Moreover, the 18-mile (29km) railway can be reached by the charming Railtrack branch line that runs from the shadows of the transporter bridge at Middlesbrough through Eskdale to Whitby. The interchange at Grosmont is almost across the platform.

If you are not arriving by rail, there is more parking space available at Pickering, and the nearby Beck Isle Museum provides an introduction to life on the North York Moors. The attractive stone station building is the first of many fine period structures on the line, including goods sheds and signal boxes. The only note of incongruity is the bizarre use of coloured light signals at Pickering.

For the first half of the one-hour journey, the railway closely follows the course of Pickering Beck through roadless Newton Dale. This unspoilt valley was scoured out by glacial action and offers walkers many opportunities, which are indicated on information boards at Levisham and Newtondale stations. Soon after the train leaves the passing loop at Levisham, the architectural folly of Skelton Tower can be seen to the right, erected by an eccentric Victorian vicar of the same name. The steep climb up the valley continues to the derelict Summit signal box at Newtondale, where passengers need to request a stop. A waymarked path leads through the woods to the west of the line back to Levisham where walkers can continue their rail journey. Beyond Newtondale the gradient eases as the train leaves the forest behind and enters a section of open moorland. To the right can be seen the early warning station at Fylingdales where the three golf-ball structures are being replaced by a pyramid.

At Eller Beck the line is crossed by the Lyke Wake Walk, which links the coast at Ravenscar with Osmotherley. The observant eye will detect traces of an abandoned railway formation on the west side of the line, which was the course of the railway until 1865 when the present line was built to eliminate a major hindrance to the railway – the inclined plane from Goathland down to Beck Hole near Grosmont. Horses and then locomotives had to haul carriages and wagons to the foot and summit of this incline, which was operated by cable powered by a stationary steam engine.

Above, passengers enjoy the glorious scenery near Grosmont

Right: Southern Railway class V 4-4-0 No 30926, Repton, *crossing the moors near Goathland*

It is well worth breaking the journey at Goathland – the station is the most attractive on the line, with some fine North Eastern Railway signals, a Historic Railway Trail leading to the route of the incline, with boards explaining its history and the significance of the remains, and for those with plenty of energy there are some of the best walks the North York Moors has to offer. A circular walk, for which boots are needed, takes you past the celebrated Mallyan Spout waterfall and one of the best-preserved stretches of Roman road, on Wheeldale Moor.

The descent of the line to Grosmont is one of the loveliest sections, dropping down through the woods and criss-crossing Eller Beck before it joins the Murk Esk at Beck Hole. The noise and smoke of ascending trains as they struggle up the fearsome 1 in 49 gradient is one of the most stirring sounds and sights to be enjoyed on a preserved railway. This is the place for some excellent photo-opportunities, with plenty of good angles for photogaphers.

As you near Goathland, the long line of the Esk Valley cottages and the trackbed of the old line can be seen to the left. Soon after, the railway's locomotive workshops and depot can be seen on the right, with a rare example of a mechanical coaling plant built since the end of steam on British railways. A whistle from the locomotive and you plunge into the double track tunnel that brings the train to journey's end and a final glimpse of the Murk Esk. Before leaving Grosmont, take a walk through Stephenson's original 1836 tunnel parallel to the newer one – it leads back to the engine shed and a viewing gallery in the workshop.

The history of this railway is particularly interesting. The Whitby & Pickering was an early line, built by the 'father of British railways', George Stephenson, and opened with the noisy celebration of five bands and 7000 people in 1836. A book in tribute to the railway was even published in the same year – *The Scenery of the Whitby & Pickering Railway* – illustrated by G H Dodgson who was apprenticed to Stephenson. Charles Dickens was amongst the early travellers on the 'quaint old railway', commenting on the use of horses for part of the way.

Train service: weekends in March, and daily from April to October. Santa specials. Tel: 01751 472508/473535.

Steam-hauled open carriages approaching Irton Road station

RAVENGLASS & ESKDALE RAILWAY
Cumbria

RAVENGLASS, 16 MILES (26 KM) SOUTH OF WHITEHAVEN

I t would be hard to quibble with the claim of the Ravenglass & Eskdale Railway that no other miniature railway in Britain passes through such magnificent scenery. Nor is that laurel likely to be taken away, since approval would never be given for such a railway today, passing as it does through the Lake District National Park for much of its length of almost 7 miles (11km). Its origins go back to 1875 when a line was opened from the old Roman port of Ravenglass

to haematite mines in Eskdale. Both mines and railway were soon in financial difficulties, but the latter soldiered on, carrying both freight and passengers until 1913.

That would have been the end of the 'Ratty', as it has long been known locally, had it not been for the Northampton model engineer and architect W J Bassett-Lowke. He leased the line, reduced the gauge from 3ft (900mm) to 15in (375mm) and re-opened it to tourists and later to

*Locomotive frames and
running gear*

stone traffic. Despite some serious ups and downs since then, its future has been secured because enough people delighted in its character, which in large measure stems from the beauty of Eskdale. The famous writer of Lake District walking books, Alfred Wainwright, regarded Eskdale as 'the finest of all valleys for those whose special joy is to travel on foot, and a paradise for artists'.

Most people begin their journey at the Ravenglass end, which can be reached by train from either Carlisle or from Carnforth and Barrow-in-Furness; both lines hug the coast and are highly recommended. The Ravenglass & Eskdale has almost taken over the main line station at Ravenglass – the main building is a pub, the Ratty Arms, the waiting room on the opposite platform is a well-presented museum about the railway's history, and the goods shed has been converted into workshops.

Trains for the 40-minute journey to Dalegarth/Eskdale leave from the adjacent three-platform station. You pass the signal box – which pioneered radio signalling in Britain – more workshops, the engine shed and the new carriage shed as the train leaves Ravenglass and heads for the first halt at Muncaster Mill. In the distance can be seen another 'first' – the world's first atomic power station at Calder Hall, now Sellafield. The River Mite accompanies the train on its approach to Muncaster Mill and farm. Flour has been ground on this site since at least 1455, though today's recently renovated structure dates from about 1700. Organic flour is now ground daily and sold to visitors.

Throughout the journey an unfolding series of panoramas of the Lakeland mountains opens up – Steeple, Pillar, Great Gable, Scafell and Scafell Pike. For the latter part of the journey Harter Fell is the dominant peak, seen in the distance to the right. The line itself passes through a mix of open pasture fringed with drystone walls and woods of birch and conifers. Bracken, gorse and heather cover some of the slopes, making this a line to beckon visitors in all seasons to experience the variety of colours.

Journey's end at Dalegarth is an opportunity to examine the locomotive as it moves on to the turntable or takes water for the return. The railway's six steam locomotives date from 1900 to 1976 and have to be capable of hauling up to 25-ton trains on the steep gradients, some as severe as 1 in 42.

2-8-2, River Esk, *built in 1923, approaching Ravenglass station*

The oldest, *Bonnie Dundee*, was built for Dundee's gasworks and has had to be regauged, but the veteran is *Synolda*. This octogenarian from Bassett-Lowke's works dates from 1912 and was the first 15in (380mm) gauge Ravenglass & Eskdale locomotive. It is used only on special occasions, lacking the power and relative youth of the other original engines.

During winter weekdays the railway journey starts from Eskdale, reflecting the importance of any public transport to the remote valley community. To operate these services the Ravenglass & Eskdale Railway has a number of diesel locomotives.

Train service: daily from Easter to October; weekends in November and February; no service in January. Santa specials in December. Tel: 01229 717171.

River Esk *'running light'* to the front of the train

A RIDE AND A WALK TO MUNCASTER

Below, the veteran Bonnie Dundee

Opposite, Northern Rock *being coaled*

*A*t the head of Eskdale lie the highest mountains in Lakeland, and at its foot are the dunes and estuary of Ravenglass. This walk incorporates a trip on a miniature railway, a water mill, a castle and a Roman ruin.

The woods of Muncaster Castle contain some very exotic trees. The castle itself is only a century old, built on to fragments of a 14th-century tower house. Walls Castle has a much better pedigree but is no more than a ruin. In fact it began as a Roman bathhouse, associated with the fort of *Glannaventa* which lies buried on the other side of the track. From the top of the hill there are fine views of Ravenglass Dunes (a nature reserve) and the Esk estuary. In the distance to the north is Sellafield Nuclear Power Station.

After the train ride, the walk is about 3 miles (5km) long, and although there are some steep sections, the walking is not difficult. There are several gates and a stile to negotiate, and short sections of road walking – one with a pavement, the other on a quiet private road.

Ravenglass is just off the A595, about 5 (8km) miles south of Gosforth. Park at the Ravenglass & Eskdale Railway and catch a train. There is an hourly service up the valley. Alight at the first stop, Muncaster Mill, and the walk starts here.

🐾🐾🐾🐾

DIRECTIONS

From Muncaster Mill station go through the mill yard and up the track, past the old wheel machinery and chicken sheds, then turn right along a bridleway, signposted 'Castle' and 'Ravenglass'. Walk along the bridleway for about 20m (22yds).

Two paths lead off to the left. Take the first of these, signposted 'Castle'. Walk up the rather steep path, through woodland, until this levels off and meets a track. Go straight on following a dip between wooded ridges for about ½ mile (0.8km). At the end of the woodland, go through a gate and turn left.

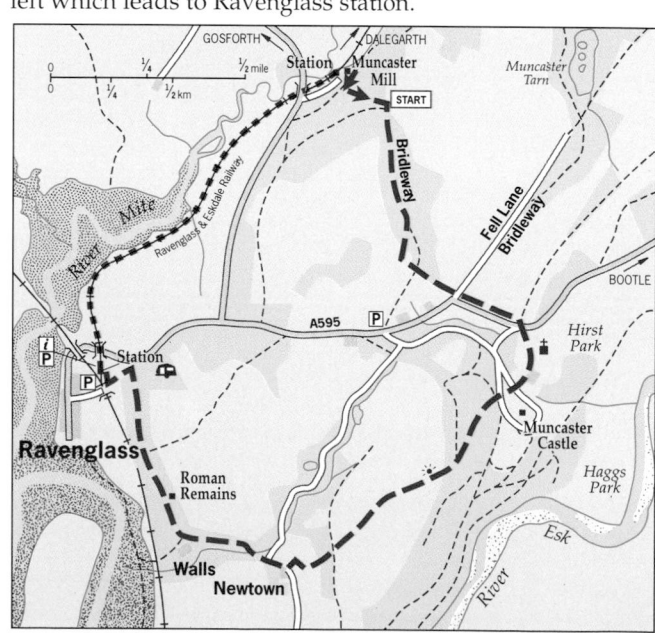

At the road (A595) go through a gate and straight on, downhill along the pavement, then cross the road with care and go through the gates of Muncaster Castle.

Walk down the drive signposted 'Muncaster Church' and 'Footpath to Ravenglass', past the stables, garden centre and café. At the end of the drive, go straight across the lawns, with waterfowl pens to your right, to meet another drive. Cross this and follow a track uphill, signposted 'Ravenglass via Newtown'. At the end of this wooded track, go over the stile and out on to the open hilltop.

The route is signposted but the path is not obvious; follow the direction indicated by the signpost, to the right of the hill crest. At isolated gate posts, continue ahead to the plantation with

the rooftops of Newtown just beyond. Cross the stile and walk downhill through the plantation to go through a gate and turn along a broad track, passing a house on the left. On reaching a metalled private road, turn right past Roman bathhouse ruins on the right, then continue to the end of the road, passing Walls Caravan Park. Just after the gates is a footpath on the left which leads to Ravenglass station.

Muncaster Mill

There has been a mill on this site since the late 15th century, and flour and oatmeal are still ground on the premises using water power from the 13ft (4m) waterwheel. The mill is open from April to September.

TANFIELD RAILWAY
County Durham

TANFIELD, 6 MILES (9.5 KM) SOUTH-WEST OF NEWCASTLE-UPON-TYNE

*F*ew preserved railways can rival the Tanfield Railway for claims to historical fame – it is the world's oldest working railway and offers passengers sight of the world's oldest surviving railway bridge. These attributes are a clue to the railway's past, for the earliest railways, usually horse-drawn wagonways, were nearly all built to carry coal, in this case from the pits of County Durham to waiting colliers on the River Tyne.

Thought to have been opened in stages between 1712 and 1725, the railway later became a steam-worked branch of the North Eastern Railway. Its industrial ancestry is perfectly reflected in the large number of industrial tank engines based at Marley Hill shed, close to the main station at Andrews House. Many operated on the dense network of colliery lines that bisected the north east. The oldest, and a regular performer on the Tanfield Railway, was built in nearby Gateshead as long ago as 1873 – few preserved railways can field such a veteran, and no other railway can match the antiquity of the Tanfield's carriages, all of which date from the 19th century.

A ride on the Tanfield Railway is a corrective to those who think of industrial landscapes as being irredeemably ugly – the section between the stone platforms and station building at Andrews House and the southern terminus at East Tanfield is through a deepening gorge lined with oak trees and a smattering of beech, ash and silver birch. It is worth getting off the train at Causey, or returning by the

Between Andrews House and Causey Arch

network of paths through the woods, to admire both the massive embankment leading to the Causey Arch and the bridge itself. When the latter was built in 1725–7, it was compared with the Via Appia, the greatest Roman road in Italy, and celebrated in prints. It is not hard to understand why people came from all over the country to see the bridge; its single 150-ft (32m) arch soars 80ft (24m) above the Causey Burn in a setting worthy of a landscape painting, and it remained the largest single-span bridge in Britain for 30 years.

The reason for the railway's preservation lies in the survival of the engine shed at Marley Hill, which until 1970 maintained locomotives from the area's colliery railways, despite the closure of the rest of the Tanfield Railway in 1962. The stone building was put up in 1855 and is thought to be the oldest engine shed in the world still fulfilling its original function. So authentic is the atmosphere in its machine shop that it has been used as a setting in the filming of a Catherine Cookson novel. Despite the complete disappearance of the surrounding coke works, colliery and rows of miners' houses at Marley Hill,

Above: Tanfield's railway yard

Left: a diesel locomotive undergoing restoration

the Tanfield Railway continues to evoke the true character of the industrial railway in a way that few other preserved railways can.

Train service: Sundays and Bank Holiday weekends from January to November; also Thursdays and Saturdays from mid-July to early September. Tel: 01207 280643.

Industrial Railways

✳

*B*efore the lorry ended almost a century of railway dominance in the carriage of goods, almost every factory, mine, quarry and port had a rail connection ranging from a single siding to an entire independent network. All over the country modest tank engines could be seen busily shuffling wagons in and out of foundries or loading bays. Both locomotives and the larger systems themselves had characters of their own, and a number of tourist railways have sought to capture something of their variety and atmosphere. The iron ore industry in Northamptonshire spawned dozens of railways to take the mineral to the nearest standard gauge railway. The Northamptonshire Ironstone Railway Trust has a museum about the industry as a whole, as well as operating a 2¼-mile (3.5km) line at Huntsbury Hill Country Park.

However, it is the coal industry that fed the railways with the lion's share of mineral traffic, and several railways perpetuate this close relationship. The most historic of these is the Middleton Railway, Leeds, which was the first

railway to be authorised by Act of Parliament (in 1758) and one of the first to adopt steam power with a pair of geared locomotives in 1812. Sadly, the 1¼-mile (2km) line perpetuates the memory of the railway rather than any physical remnant, but the fine collection of locomotives operates on a similar route.

One of the most intriguing operations to be witnessed on any preserved railway is that on the Bowes Railway, Gateshead, where the working of inclined planes is demonstrated. The steep hills of County Durham made impossible the construction of conventional railways, so cables controlled the ascent and descent of wagons up steep slopes. The cables are wound round large drums powered by electric winding engines, though stationary steam engines were once used. The manual detaching of the cable as a string of wagons breasts the summit requires skill and dexterity – and the Bowes Railway is the only place in Britain where this once common operation is still demonstrated.

Below and right, among former industrial locomotives on the Middleton Railway is one imported tank engine, an 0-4-0WT built in 1895 by Hartmann in Chemnitz; No 385 spent its earlier life on the docks in Denmark

Finally, there is a conventional preserved railway that has almost no locomotives from any background other than industry. The Embsay Steam Railway operates 2 miles (3km) of the former Midland Railway from Skipton in the Dales, but its trains are worked by nothing larger than a six-wheeled tank engine, its oldest four-coupled tank dating from 1908.

BO'NESS & KINNEIL RAILWAY

Falkirk

BO'NESS, 15 MILES (24 KM) WEST OF EDINBURGH

Bo'ness West station; its recreated buildings have won several awards

The closure of railways in Britain has seldom been accompanied by sensible provisions to safeguard the integrity of the trackbed and structures in case they were needed again. None the less, most railway preservation schemes were on the scene quickly enough to prevent the principal buildings being demolished or sold off. A notable exception was the Bo'ness & Kinneil Railway on the southern shore of the Firth of Forth – when the preservationists began work, they lacked even the remains of the trackbed or any foundations on which to rebuild a working railway.

It is a measure of their achievement that Bo'ness station deceives most visitors into thinking that it is the original. The setting is striking: inland the town of stone buildings rises up the hillside, crowned by the villas of the more well-to-do; seaward are the remains of the harbour on which the town's wealth was largely based. At one time 11 miles (17.6km) of sidings covered the waterfront, the wagons filled with coal for export or with

'Maude'

Acting the part...

imported iron ore and timber. Today the site is home to the largest collection of locomotives, carriages and wagons in Scotland, where most of them were built or worked.

The building that commands admiration is the huge cast- and wrought-iron train shed built in 1842 for Haymarket station in Edinburgh. The rescue of what is one of the finest buildings on any preserved railway was part of the intention to re-create an authentic North British Railway station – that pre-grouping company owned the 4½-mile (7km) line that linked Bo'ness with the Edinburgh–Glasgow main line at Manuel. Before boarding the train, it is worth taking the visitor trail round the goods yard with its wagon turntables, used in restricted sites, and through the vast shed that houses much of the collection.

Pride of place amongst the carriages must go to the Great North of Scotland Railway saloon which was once part of Edward VII's royal train. However, most of the carriages illustrate just how spartan travelling conditions were for third-class passengers until the early years of this century. Locomotives range from main line passenger engines to humble industrial tank engines from the days when large factories and works would be rail connected and have a 'pug', as they were called in Scotland, fussing round the yard.

The booking office at Bo'ness

The start of the 3½-mile (5.5km) journey to Birkhill, the present terminus of the line, passes the dock on the right before the train meanders through a plantation of saplings that now covers the foreshore. Kinneil Halt is used by birdwatchers visiting the adjacent bird sanctuary on the headland. The line forges inland, the deepening bark from the locomotive's exhaust indicating the rising gradient. As the line enters a woodland of ivy-clad trees, it passes close to Kinneil House where an outbuilding was the scene of James Watt's experiments to produce more efficient steam engines.

The ugly sight of Grangemouth oil refinery across the Firth soon disappears from view as the line swings inland and crosses the site of the Antonine Wall, built by the Romans as a bulwark against invasion by the Caledonians. A mile of pastoral landscape precedes arrival at Birkhill, a remote station seemingly offering visitors nothing more than the pretty station building with its oversized cast-iron brackets supporting the canopy. However, simply to return by the next train would be to miss one of the most interesting experiences to be had from a journey on a preserved railway. Behind the station, hidden by trees, are the remains of the boiler house of Birkhill Clay Mine – unremarkable to all except industrial archaeologists, but beyond is an extraordinary sight. The ground drops away to reveal a precipitous gorge through which the River Avon flows.

A long flight of steps parallels a rope-worked inclined plane which hauled small wagons, called hutches, up the hillside from the mine in the valley floor. At the bottom a bridge over the river leads to the mine entrance. The 6 miles (9.6km) of tunnel were worked as recently as 1980, and retired miners now take parties through some of the workings. Hundreds of feet below the ground torches can pick out the remains of tree trunks that were fossils 170 million years before the first dinosaurs. What was extracted from the mine was turned into firebricks capable of withstanding very high temperatures. They were used in many industries, not least in locomotive fireboxes. The driver of the locomotive that takes your train back to Bo'ness may let you see the brick arch in the firebox, making an immediate link with the mine and the guide's personal recollections.

Train service: at weekends from April to mid-October; and daily from mid-July to end August. Santa specials. Tel: 01506 822298.

Below No 2392 arriving at Bo'ness

The railway's purpose was to take visitors arriving from Oban to Torosay Castle

MULL & WEST HIGHLAND NARROW GAUGE RAILWAY
Argyll & Bute

CRAIGNURE, ISLE OF MULL, NEAR FERRY LANDING FROM OBAN

Most miniature gauge railways are purely for fun, and often run in circuits. The man credited with their invention, Sir Arthur Heywood, envisaged them being useful for estate or military purposes, but he would have approved of the 10¼in (260mm) gauge Mull & West Highland Railway – Scotland's only island railway connects with the ferry from Oban to take passengers to one of the island's principal tourist attractions, the mid 19th-century Torosay Castle. The connections are generous, allowing passengers half an hour to find their land legs and saunter along the front.

The idea for the railway stemmed from the difficulty the castle's owners were having in persuading people to walk the 2 miles (3km) from the pier. A group of promoters was formed and surveying began. Part of the route uses an old carriage drive that was built in the 1850s between the castle and the pier but never used, because the Kirk refused to allow it to cross church land for the final part. It was so overgrown

with rhododendrons 120 years later that the survey had to be done on hands and knees, but the colours in early summer are now one of the railway's attractions.

In complete contrast to the secluded character of the carriage drive is the first section of the line, which enjoys spectacular views over the Sound of Mull to Ben Nevis, the Glencoe Hills and the Island of Lismore. A stop at a loop named Tarmstedt is an opportunity for passengers to watch the engine take water. Its naming after a German town is due to a former owner of Torosay, who was also the first chairman of the Mull & West Highland; he began two escape attempts from a German prison camp at that narrow gauge station – the second was successful.

Another curious link that the railway has is with the Puffing Billy Railway in Victoria, Australia. The search for a suitable prototype on which to base the Mull & West Highland's third locomotive ended with a set of plans of a tank engine used on the best-known tourist railway in the Antipodes. The result is now thought to be the largest tank engine of 10¼in (260mm) gauge in the world, which can haul 11 carriages with 190 passengers for the 20-minute journey.

Train service: during the Easter holiday, then daily from late April to mid-October. Tel: 01680 812494.

Getting Lady of the Isles *ready for action*

Main Line Steam Operations

✳

*T*here was a time in the early 1970s, when the last years of steam locomotives on main line railways were a recent memory, that their use on special trains was prohibited, except for one engine – *Flying Scotsman*. An earlier agreement between British Rail and the famous locomotive's owner, Alan Pegler, allowed it to run several excursions, including the epic non-stop run from London to Edinburgh which the BBC made into a fine documentary.

The arrival of Sir Richard Marsh as Chairman of British Rail in 1971 heralded a complete turn around, and it was accepted that British Rail was losing both goodwill and revenue from its obdurate position. The return to the main line of some of the many large steam locomotives in private hands was a milestone. Some of these engines were unsuitable for use on lightly engineered preserved railways, and there is a huge difference between the spectacle of an express train of a dozen coaches hurtling along on a main line and the typical preserved railway train of half the length ambling through the countryside.

For two decades now private steam locomotives have been giving pleasure to millions, and adding millions to British Rail's accounts. It hasn't all been plain sailing, of course – stringent and sometimes costly safety checks had to be made by official inspectors on a regular basis, and all the trappings of the steam age had been ripped out with great haste, so water columns or hydrants, coaling arrangements and turning facilities or even turntables have to be organised. To simplify matters selected routes were approved for steam running, with one-off exceptions to mark a special anniversary. The most popular have been the famous Settle & Carlisle line and the equally lovely route between Fort William and Mallaig. The latter has proved so popular that regular daily trains have run during the summer months since 1984.

Although all liaison with main line operators has had to be through the Steam Locomotive Owners' Association, the individual excursions have been organised by different societies, so there is no central marketing of them. The only way to find out about all the various special

The famous Glenfinnan viaduct, over 1000ft (300m) long, on the West Highland Line at the head of Loch Shiel

trains is to peruse the pages of one of the monthly railway magazines with a bent towards steam. Although the steam sections are in relatively rural parts of the country, most excursions start behind electric or diesel power from a major city.

Usually there are good opportunities for passengers to admire the engine as it takes water, though the frequency of service on most lines has so far made impossible to organise on a regular basis the run-pasts which are a normal part of such occasions in the United States. These are scrupulously organised events, in which photographers can leave the train, which then backs down the line under instruction from organisers with radios. At a given signal, the locomotive accelerates the train past the photographers, who are tidily lined up to give everyone a clear view. It then backs down to pick them up before proceeding on its way.

Most of the locomotives with main line certificates are based at working museums, or on a preserved railway, so they can be seen at other times.

Leaving Glenfinnan station. The West Highland Line, built to serve the fishing trade, is one of Scotland's most popular tourist routes

STRATHSPEY RAILWAY
Highland

AVIEMORE, 29 MILES (46.5 KM) SOUTH OF INVERNESS

*T*his line follows the valley of the River Spey, with the Cairngorm Mountains rising to the south-east. Since the growth of winter sports in Scotland during the late 1960s, Aviemore has become the major centre for skiing, a network of chairlifts serving slopes around the small town. Until then it was known for little more than being an important junction on the railway between Perth and Inverness, where trains went either directly to Inverness over Slochd summit or took the circuitous route through Forres and Nairn. Passenger services over the latter were withdrawn in 1965, but preservationists and the Highlands & Islands Development Board wanted to save the 5-mile (8km) section between Aviemore and the tranquil village of Boat of Garten.

Their efforts came to fruition in 1978 when regular services were resumed during the tourist season. Unfortunately Strathspey Railway trains are unable to run into the main line station, but it is only a short walk between the two. The Strathspey has created an authentic feel to its Aviemore station by re-erecting railway buildings of the former Highland and Great North of Scotland railways, which served the area before the 1922 grouping. It has one of the finest locomotive sheds on any preserved railway – a solid stone four-track shed, which became a garage after its closure in around 1966

All ship-shape at Boat of Garten station on the Speyside line

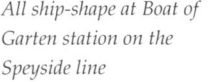

but was returned to its rightful use by the Strathspey Railway, and it can be seen to the east as the train pulls out of Aviemore for the 20-minute journey.

Once over a level crossing serving the holiday village at Dalfaber, the line is into open country with fine views of the Cairngorm mountains to the east and the Monadhliaths to the west. Clumps of trees sometimes indicate surviving remnants of the Caledonian Forest that once covered the area. Silver birches accompany the approach to Boat of Garten, where it is worth spending some time.

The former junction for the Speyside line to Craigellachie today offers a railway museum, and the Strathspey Railway's excellent guide book suggests two walks from the station. You can also take a vintage coach to an observation hide provided by the Royal Society for the Protection of Birds that overlooks Loch Garten; since the 1950s this has been home to ospreys that have returned here each year from their winter refuge in Africa.

Train service: daily from June to September, most days in April, May and October. Santa specials. Tel: 01479 810725.

No doubt as to the owners of this handsome locomotive here at Aviemore

INDEX